ESSAYS IN POETRY

MAINLY AUSTRALIAN

VINCENT BUCKLEY

ESSAYS IN POETRY

MAINLY AUSTRALIAN

Essay Index Reprint Series

BOOKS FOR LIBRARIES PRESS

FREEPORT, NEW YORK

First published by Melbourne University Press, 1957

Reprinted 1969 by arrangement

PR 9471
B 8

STANDARD BOOK NUMBER:

8369-1174-1

LIBRARY OF CONGRESS CATALOG CARD NUMBER:

77-86738

PRINTED IN THE UNITED STATES OF AMERICA

Acknowledgments

The author wishes to express his thanks to the following for permission to reprint copyright material:

David Campbell for the extract from 'As I was going through Windy Gap'; the author and Messrs Chatto and Windus for the extract from David Campbell's *Speak with the Sun;* the author and Messrs Angus and Robertson for the extracts by Hugh McCrae; the author and Messrs Angus and Robertson for the extracts from Kenneth Slessor's *100 Poems;* the author and Messrs Angus and Robertson for extracts from Judith Wright's *Woman to Man, The Gateway,* and *The Two Fires;* Judith Wright for extracts from *The Moving Image;* the author and Messrs Angus and Robertson for the extracts from Douglas Stewart's works; the author and Melbourne University Press for extracts from R. D. FitzGerald's *Moonlight Acre* and *This Night's Orbit;* R. D. FitzGerald for the extract from *To Meet the Sun;* Faber and Faber for extracts from T S. Eliot's *Collected Poems, 1909-1925;* also for extract from Norman Nicholson's 'Michaelmas'; also extract from W. H. Auden's *Collected Shorter Poems;* David Gascoyne for extract from *Poems, 1937-1942;* Messrs J. M. Dent for extract from Dylan Thomas' *Collected Poems;* the author and Messrs Pearn, Pollinger and Higham for extracts from John Manifold's *Selected Poems,* published by Dennis Dobson; Messrs Pearn, Pollinger and Higham for the extract from Dame Edith Sitwell's 'The Coat of Fire'; R. G. Howarth for the extract from *Notes on Modern Poetic Technique: English and Australian;* the author and Messrs Edwards and Shaw for extracts from A. D. Hope's *The Wandering Islands;* the author and Messrs Edwards and Shaw for extracts from *Thirty Poems,* by John Thompson; the author and Melbourne University Press for extracts from *Under Aldebaran,* by James McAuley; the author for extracts from *A Vision of Ceremony;* Messrs Faber and Faber for the extracts from the works of Vernon Watkins and George Barker; Ray Mathew for the extracts from *To Cyprus Pine* and *Song and Dance;* the author and Messrs

Angus and Robertson for extract from Nancy Keesing's *Three Men and Sydney;* Nancy Cato for the extract from *The Dancing Bough;* Laurence Collinson for the extracts from *Poet's Dozen;* Messrs Angus and Robertson for the extracts from 'The Wanderer' by Christopher Brennan, and for the extracts from Henry Lawson's works; Elizabeth Riddell for 'Country Tunes'; Lothian Publishing Company for the extract from Bernard O'Dowd's 'Dawnward'.

Contents

Preface

THESE ESSAYS are mainly about Australian poetry. Some of them are about nothing else, and of these the majority are concerned with the development of our poetry over the last thirty years. One or two, however, are concerned with local poetry in the context of recent poetic developments in England and elsewhere. I cannot apologize for such an emphasis; for I think it essential that our poetry be seen, not perhaps as part of an overseas movement, but at least against the background of such a movement.

Some readers may feel that my relationship with Australian poetry is characterized by a strain of *odi et amo;* they may think me too harsh, too critical of a literature which is still in bud; they may find blame treading too hard on the heels of a too-scrawny praise – indeed, on its very instep. And I *am* conscious, on reading the first half-dozen essays, of having given grounds for such a supposition; I have probably not spoken strongly enough of my love for the best of our poetry, and of my hopes for its development. One castigates where one's emotions are most deeply engaged. And more than this: one must not let one's hopes be founded on an unrealistic or irrational assessment of the possibilities. In many of these essays, I have stated my belief in what has already been achieved in this country – so much so that people who despise the local scene may find my enthusiasm merely silly. I believe in our poetry; but I also believe that its development is being thwarted by influences within our literary tradition as well as by influences outside it, in society as a whole. That belief provides some reason for the harshness and apparent dogmatism.

'Never apologize; never explain,' said Jowett; yet these things require some explanation, even if they need no apology. The essays which follow do have a thesis running through them, a thesis in which my view of poetry and of its social function is at least implied. That thesis might have been clearer had all the essays been written at the same time and under the same conditions. But they were not. Some were written as I felt a personal need to write them; some were written to editorial requirements; some were prepared to be delivered as lectures. Therefore, they repeat and overlap one another; many considerations are left out, which might otherwise have gone in; certain worthwhile poets are omitted, or have been treated more cursorily than I like.

This fact, which has had an influence on their content, has influenced their form as well. Some of them bear the marks of their origin as lectures, marks which only a deep incision could have cut out; others are as obviously written to the requirements of magazine publication. Such details are no doubt minor, and I mention them in order to forestall misunderstanding.

My thanks are due not only to the poets about whom I have written, and whose works have in many cases pleased and taught me so much, but also to others: To the editors of *Meanjin, Twentieth Century, Melbourne University Magazine,* and *Direction,* in which some of the items first appeared, sometimes in a slightly different form; to the Departments of English at the Universities of Melbourne and Sydney, where some of them were given as lectures under the Commonwealth Literary Fund. These authorities have readily given me permission to re-print.

My particular thanks are due to Professor Ian Maxwell, of the University of Melbourne, who has encouraged their publication, and to A. D. Hope who, in the character of professor rather than poet, has encouraged the writing of several of them.

The Image of Man in Australian Poetry

POETRY CONCERNS itself with the image of man; there is nothing else worthy of its attention, nothing else which it is so eminently fitted to reflect. Perhaps such a statement may be made about any of the major arts; yet in every art the aspect of man which is reflected is obviously connected in some intimate way with the typical forms, pressures, and manners of the art itself. And with poetry, which is so versatile, which can do so many things, which is so abiding a force in human society, it is difficult to say what aspect of man is central to its various movements and formations.

At any rate we can, I believe, give a number of hints. I believe that the central human concern of poetry is not, as it is with painting, the external actions of man, or the physical dispositions of the human face and figure; it is not, as it is with fiction, the social relationships or the psychological intricacies of human life. If I say that poetry deals with man at a metaphysical level, I am inviting misunderstanding; yet such a proposition would seem to be broadly true. Poetry deals with man at a metaphysical level – but with man's metaphysical status reflected in his actual state, localized in his actual physical surroundings, embodied in his sensuous and spiritual reactions to his world. It strikes to the meaning and not the detail of man's life. The complex of signs which we find in any really fine poem is a symbol of man's metaphysical state presented through whatever in fact is most real to him as a suffering and diurnal being.

This is not offered as a definition of poetry *tout court;* it is offered, rather, as the intellectual background against which I propose to investigate the varying attempts to portray the human in Australian poetry; and I had better anticipate something of my later remarks by putting at the outset a few general considerations.

There is something tribal, something even primitive, about Australian poetry; in speaking so, I am speaking not of its imagery but of its range of subjects and allusions. It is impossible to locate in it the varying conceptions of man which it has entertained, without relating them to the varying reactions which, over the past century, Australian poets have had to the land itself. The myths which have dominated our poetry, frail and indeterminate though they may be, have been myths of nature as well as of man; they have reflected a struggle for the acclimatization of the senses before the adequate placing of the spirit. They have developed apart from any firm philosophical position, and quite outside the ambit of any explicitly religious vision. They are therefore incomplete, question-begging, and crude. Yet they are none the less susceptible of a friendly analysis.

The tradition of Australian poetry, as of Australian society, has been an anti-intellectual one. Many commentators will agree that the level of intellectual aspiration in Australian life is not very imposing. We are always for localizing the truth, for assuming the answers to the basic questions about man's life or for answering them in a casual, pragmatic, workaday manner. If our religion is vaguely pantheist, concerned with works rather than with faith, our philosophy is social, concerned with consolidating human relations rather than with understanding them. From the pragmatism of the pioneers, those who had a set of immediate tasks to perform, we have passed to a pragmatism of the consolidators, those who have an immediate experience to undergo. In a settled and prosperous land such as this, only a tiny minority asks itself the central questions about the destiny of all. And the poets are not always members of this minority. For us, poetry is not a vocation, but an additional pleasure; it is not a seeing of ultimate meanings, but a surrender to immediate experiences, whether sensuous, emotional, or even intellectual. The life of the mind is merely one among others in a range of possible experiences.

Such an analysis may be regarded either as insulting or as commonplace; in either case, I am half-ashamed to have to repeat it. But these ideas will bear restatement; my justification for repeating them is that I believe them to be true; and if they *are* true, they indicate the pressing nature of the problem of the arts in Australia, and they indicate too the lines on which a solution is to be sought. They provide, therefore, the intellectual climate in which my present discussion takes place, and from which it gets its sharpness – a sharpness which may well be found too harsh and dogmatic.

Any culture or society shows its attitude to man, one might almost say its humanism, in what it believes and in how it acts – that is, in its philosophy, its morals, and its social institutions. Poets, on the other hand, have subtler methods; for them, attitudes to man are expressed, embodied in their dominant images, their symbols, their emotional relations, their tone and rhythm, in all that enables them to wed ideas to poetic form. And we shall frequently find that a poet's central attitude to the human image is to be found in his attitude to himself; his awareness of his own destiny contains what he thinks of his fellowmen. That is the real reason why it is a mistake to impose on art the regularity, the static perfection, of a philosophy.

We hear little nowadays about the glories of Australian poetry in the nineteenth century; perhaps many of us have decided that the glories never existed. We have cut ourselves off, in short, from the views typical of most of that century; and in doing so we have probably cut ourselves off from most of its poetry as well. Our poetry up to (say) the nineties of last century did not represent the Australian landscape or the Australian people in anything like the same way, or to anything like the same degree, as does the best of our modern poetry. It could not represent the human and 'natural' surroundings of Australian man because it was the product of a non-Australian mentality and sensibility. As so many critics have insisted, these poets were un-Australian in a crippling sense; they were aliens, with the imaginations of *émigrés;* and they were, in consequence, most imperfectly awakened to the poetic possibilities of the land itself, of the people, even of their own thoughts and emotions. After all, a man whose imagination is cut off from the life around him is almost inevitably cut off from certain aspects of himself as well.

From those quite remarkably infelicitous men, Barron Field and Michael Massey Robinson, right down the century to Henry Kendall and even Victor Daley, we have a poetry of the Anglicizers, the unassimilable, we might almost call them the poetically unemployable. And in almost every case we find not so much a poetry solid for the most part but in some way flawed, as a poetry stunted, ruined, irremediably softened at its source. What, then, was the cause? It is beyond all reason to conclude that any country, even a colony, could have as one of its main primary products one hundred years of poor verse without some counterbalancing virtues.

The reason is that it was not a primary product at all; it was a secondary product. I suppose that my putting the matter in this way generates the uneasy feeling that I am about to raise the slogan 'Buy Australian goods only', or to drag a whole race of versifiers before a committee for the investigation of un-Australian imaginations. It would be foolish and impertinent to do anything of either sort. It is not a question (and I emphasize it now) whether or not poets ought to conform to some arbitrary ideal of Australianness; it is rather a question what kind of humanism, what attitude to human problems, what conception of artistic composition, can be expected from men dabbling their feet in an imaginative void.

In the case we are considering it was, of course, a humanism dominated completely by the emotional fact of exile. If we ask how Robinson and Field, or Daley and Gordon saw the land, the answer is that they did not see it at all; they conceptualized it instead, and when they came to look on their own concepts, they did not at all like what they looked on. If we ask how they saw the people, we must answer that, on the whole, they did not see a people at all; they saw themselves, and they saw the 'natives'. It is the Anglo-Indian complex transported to Australia, in parody of that earlier transportation which most of these men would have been the first to deride.

This, no doubt, is a generalization wider than most people would care to make; yet I believe it to be in essence a true one. The terms in which most of the nineteenth-century writers saw Australia, the physical and social presence of Australia, are a reflection of the terms in which they saw their own aspirations; and these aspirations on the whole were such that Australia could not be seen as a home, and so not as a complete goad to, and context for, the poetic spirit.

The Anglicizers tended to divide into two types. First, there were the 'activists', men who, whether or not they were men of action or of active temperament, saw Australia as a field for adventure, an open place which no imagination had yet peopled or furnished, and into which Englishness could be carried with impunity. By Englishness I mean the English idea of adventure together with the ideal of the Englishman comporting himself in a foreign land, an ideal of duty, excitement, and etiquette all together. But the land itself was presented to them as having no poetic substance, its details of landscape and of social living did not appear to be natural materials for the poetic sensibility to feed on. It was no more and no less than a field for action; and hence there could be in these adventurers no strong and constant urge to identify themselves with the aspirations of the people who were native to it.

All this is more obviously true of the novelists, such as Kingsley and Marcus Clarke, than of the poets. But if we look at the poetry of Harpur or Adam Lindsay Gordon we shall see its truth peeping forth in every touch of the poetic texture. In 'The Sick Stockrider', allegedly one of Gordon's more Australian poems, we see that, although Australia seems to him a place to adventure in, even to die in, it is not a place fully to live in, not a presence or a home, not the local habitation to which words give its final reality:

> For good undone, and gifts misspent, and resolutions vain,
> 'Tis somewhat late to trouble. This I know —
> I should live the same life over, if I had to live again;
> And the chances are I go where most men go.
>
> The deep blue skies wax dusky and the tall green trees grow
> dim,
> The sward beneath me seems to heave and fall;
> And sickly, smoky shadows through the sleepy sunlight swim,
> And on the very sun's face weave their pall.
>
> Let me slumber in the hollow where the wattle blossoms wave,
> With never stone or rail to fence my bed;
> Should the sturdy station children pull the bush flowers on
> my grave
> I may chance to hear them romping overhead.

This is the typical note of the adventurous young man whose adventuring is done; a note of bravado, nostalgia, and determined resignation, all suspiciously like the attitude to life of Kingsley's heroes, whom Joseph Furphy characterized as 'slender-witted, virgin-souled, overgrown schoolboys'. Gordon deserves better of us than a characterization such as this; nevertheless, the point is, or ought to be, instructive.

That, at any rate, seems to me to be one side of the Anglicizer's coin, the side of adventure and English manliness. The other side is that of introspection and of nature mysticism, in which the dominant note is one of nostalgia and defeat. Gordon may again be cited as an example. But, indeed, it is the most constant strain of *émigré* poetry in the last century, from Robinson and Field through Harpur and even later poets. Again, it comes largely from the fact that Australia was not seen as in any sense a spiritual home. Beneath their verses, whether languid or lilting, we feel continually the throb of the Biblical lament: 'By the waters of Babylon we sat down and wept: for we remembered thee, O Sion.' Remembered, that is, nineteenth-century England. But no man can engage in introspection in a vacuum. There is no such thing as a purely mental poetry. What the person apprehends of himself in the process of poetry must be apprehended through sensuous images, and cannot help being heightened, given richness and overtone, by the emotional context which those images provide. So in Harpur and Gordon we tend to get a generalized, vague, impressionistic landscape either of an England which they had almost forgotten, or of an Australia which they were not yet in a position to see. We get, too, the vices of emotional vagueness, over-exaggeration, and an unconvincing melancholy. Because there seemed to be no source of fruitfulness in the life around them, they imitated facile English rhythms. Even Henry Kendall, an Australian born on the spot, did so, and gave us the amazing anomaly of an Australian with an almost completely English sensibility. But Kendall had a literary mind; he saw the Australian landscape, certainly, and he had no other landscape with which to compare it; but he saw it almost purely in terms of the English preRaphaelite poetry with which his reading had so completely saturated his mind and senses:

No longer doth the earth reveal
Her gracious green and gold;
I sit where youth was once, and feel
That I am growing old.
The lustre from the face of things
Is wearing all away;
Like one who halts with tired wings
I rest and muse to-day.

There is a river in the range
I love to think about;
Perhaps the searching feet of change
Have never found it out.
Ah! oftentimes I used to look
Upon its banks, and long
To steal the beauty of that brook
And put it in a song.

I wonder if the slopes of moss,
In dreams so dear to me –
The falls of flower, and flower-like floss –
Are as they used to be!
I wonder if the waterfalls,
The singers far and fair,
That gleamed between the wet, green walls,
Are still the marvels there.

The grace and poignancy of this cannot be doubted; yet how completely lacking in substance, in individuality, are all the items in his catalogue of beauties. The reason is that they are literary properties rather than present things. There is no pressure in them or in the mind which knows them. Kendall's moods are real, and their expression musical, but he conveys to us little of their individuality, little of their humanity, of their meaning, of their sensuous context.

By the eighties of last century, the transplanted English approach was beginning to be replaced with something more vital, with a different view of man's endeavours and of the meaning which Australia confers on them. The reason which is almost always advanced to account for the change in literary attitude is that a profound change was taking place in social attitudes, and that this change, in turn, derived from a re-ordering of the social forces in the country. I cannot subscribe to such an interpretation; it is too simple, and it ignores too many of the facts. Still, it is true that the last two decades of the century were the decades of the democrats, many of whom were also fiercely Australian. We cannot help recalling Furphy's tag 'Bias, offensively Australian', and we remember that there were appearing both native Australian poets and a completely new kind of exile. Victor Daley is an example of the latter, as Lawson, Brennan, and O'Dowd are examples of the former. Daley was not an Englishman, he was an Irishman; he was not upper class, he was lower middle class; he was not an adventurer, he was a Bohemian wanderer; he was not a professional exile, he was a dreamer and a democrat. And we find ourselves taking to Daley as to one of ourselves, in a way that we cannot quite take to Gordon and Harpur. His was a mind soaked in the strictly ersatz mists of the Celtic Twilight; but he wrote a different kind of poetry as well – the poetry of social protest associated with his nom-de-plume, Creeve Roe. And Daley is an instructive case. Much of his poetry was, of course, personal fantasy, and it is true that he did not use it to identify himself with a peculiarly nationalist aspiration of the Australian people. But there was a class aspiration for him to identify himself with, and he did identify himself with it. The humanism of Daley, like that of Lawson and Quinn, was a humanism of class feeling, of brotherhood joined in a definite struggle. In him man the ineffective dreamer met (but did not quite join) man the realistic rebel. Australia was viewed as at once a land of unbounded opportunity, and a land in which aspirations not only legitimate, but noble, were being thwarted by social forces. Moreover it was an inhabited land, a land with human prints on it, a society; and the people which worked in it was seen as being in some way proper to it.

These were the 'democrat' poets, then, seeing more of Australian society than their predecessors did, putting themselves and their poetry in tune with the hidden movements of that society, and fiercely insisting that they were humanists.

I do not want to over-emphasize this, for in Daley and Lawson we still get a constant note of exile or of alienation; and they are, after all, poetically divided personalities. Their view was, in the last resort, a narrow one, an insufficiently imaginative one because it was centred on too small a range of human

affairs. Many of them wrote for the *Bulletin,* and therefore to a
largely outback audience. They had a small range of emotions,
embodied in a small and insufficiently resonant range of verse
forms, tending to an uneasy cross between the ballad and the
lyric; and their social and philosophical ideas were incomplete
and crude. They saw and reflected too little, in f..ct, of Australian
life; they constituted a sort of working-class Bohemia. We see
their spirit fleshed, for instance, in the stirring but tentative
verse of Henry Lawson:

> Ah, then their hearts were bolder,
> And if Dame Fortune frowned,
> Their swags they'd lightly shoulder
> And tramp to other ground.
> Oh, they were lion-hearted
> Who gave our country birth!
> Stout sons, of stoutest fathers born,
> From all the lands on earth!
>
> Those golden days are vanished,
> And altered is the scene;
> The diggings are deserted,
> The camping-grounds are green;
> The flaunting flag of progress
> Is in the West unfurled;
> The mighty Bush with iron rails
> Is tethered to the world.

This is simple, crude, narrow; and yet it is hard to resist the
temporary excitement when one reads it. Looking back from
the perspective afforded by the present, we may say that all
these men made a semi-conscious attempt to acclimatize themselves to Australia by constructing a group myth about Australians and their destiny. I must admit that if Lawson himself
were to hear me say as much, he would probably dismiss it as
one of the more pretentious sayings of the 'literary men' whom
he detested so much. Yet some such attempt was made; and
the manner in which it was made presupposed a certain image
of man and his meaning. In reacting against the *émigré* view
of Australia and her citizens, Lawson and his friends revolted as
well against the conceptions of class responsibility and culture
which had made such a view possible. They were recovering Aus-

tralia for Australian man as they knew him; and Australian man
as they knew him was a man susceptible of only the more rudi-
mentary forms of poetic expression. Their view, then, was one
which, in its very insistence on freedom, became in the end a
cramp and a limitation on poetry. Out of it sprang the beginnings of that nationalism which in its various forms and disguises was to dominate so much of our literary scene over the
past sixty years, and which was to find so many avatars, some of
them inept, some of them men of a divided allegiance, some of
them merely and insistently silly.

The Australian critic, A. G. Stephens, once made a remark
about Lawson which is applicable to most of Lawson's colleagues
as well. He said: '[Lawson] seems to have used all his vivid
objective impressions without replacing them by subjective ideas
of equal literary significance'. This seems to me to indicate the
essential defect in their vision; it is not a matter peculiar to Lawson, but common to his times; in fact, the relationship between
objective and subjective within their work was too tenuous to
ensure a poetic vision. One feels that all the optimism, melancholy, moral indignation of these men are not sufficiently related
to a personal vision of man and nature. Whatever joy, whatever
pathos are bestowed, are bestowed on the external affairs of man,
apply to the thwarting of man's social function. Their ideas
(though noble) are too circumscribed, their feelings (though
genuine) too exterior. It was all not of a 'sufficiently literary significance'. If mateship is the central value, then nostalgia cannot
help being its central emotional equivalent. And nostalgia is the
most deceptive of all sentiments for literature. It seems the most
poetic, and is in fact the least; and, if too constantly indulged
in, it weakens the poetic vision beyond repair.

Vision is the very quality which the most notable of the later
poets strove to attain. Brennan, O'Dowd, McCrae, and Baylebridge were men less interested in life as they conceived men in
general to live it than in life as it may be refined and strengthened
in the interior fires of the imagination and will. To that extent,
they are on the side of poetry and against that of cant. None of
them was a balladist, none (with the possible exception of McCrae)
primarily a lyrist; they were all rhetoricians. We have in their
work something of an age of rhetoric – rhetoric in the cause of

nationalism, of soul-searching, of metaphysics, or of a wide pagan joy. O'Dowd, perhaps the most famous of them, but by no means the best of them, saw man in the abstract, and attempted to prescribe for him. Though politically O'Dowd was advanced, poetically he was a reactionary, an arthritic yet ambitious Shelley chanting of the fabulous destiny of Australian man, and attempting to show that destiny as part of the wider glory to which the land itself was destined. Yet, despite his very real concern for human affairs, neither man nor the land comes very convincingly into his poetry. The language is abstract and unrhythmic, clogged with cerebral images and harsh classicisms :

> They seek no dim-eyed mob's applause,
> Deem base the titled name,
> And spurn, for glory of their Cause,
> The tawdry nymphs of Fame.
>
> No masks of ignorance or sin
> Hide from them you or me :
> We're Man — no colour shames our skin,
> No race or caste have we.
>
> The prognathous Neanderthal,
> To them, conceals the Bruce;
> They see Dan Aesop in the thrall;
> From swagmen Christ deduce.

The sentiment is admirable, but nothing in its expression savours of poetic reality. Everything is generalized, opaque; nothing is given its local habitation or due name. The attempt is neither ignoble nor negligible, but it accomplishes nothing of what its author intended – the making real, in poetic terms, of man's aspiration to live freely and in brotherhood. The democracy of the woolsheds had been easy to express, because there was not much to it. O'Dowd's democracy, however, is neither empirical nor utilitarian; it is an attempt to realize in human society a mystical doctrine, but to do so without calling on anything of that sensuous life, that loving and expressive particularity, which is the poet's own way of declaring his concern for his brothers, and without which his declaration must

remain ineffective. O'Dowd's work may be quite admirable; it is
seldom poetry.

The same vices beset Baylebridge's personal manifestos.
Brennan, however, is a different case. It is true that his rhetoric
is a solitary, even an individualistic one; and it is true that his
poetry is cerebral, his images general, and his view of man's
plight a metaphysical one – a view of man exiled from Eden. At
the same time, this self-centred poetry gives a vision of every
man's soul in its despair and exultation, gives a measure of
man's aspiration to be not only free in society, but intact within
himself. That is where Brennan excels the others, and his partial
success is reflected in the relative flexibility of his rhythms as
in the symbolic power which his main images take on. Unlike
the others, he is fighting out the quarrel with himself, as Yeats
bade, and he is making of it poetry – poetry of a rhetorical kind.
It is the first and best emergence in Australian poetry of the
depth and the universality of man's struggle with himself and
his destiny. And it is by no means a solipsistic poetry, as it may at
first appear. Brennan's range of practical reference is wide. City
life comes into it, landscapes of sea as well as bush; it is full
of subtle evocations of the detailed presence of Australia. For,
more than most of the others, Brennan felt at home here – as
much at home as he could feel anywhere; he could at least
assume the presence of the land as the natural context for the
working out of his personal yet typical struggle, the natural
repository of images to heighten and focus the passion of that
struggle.

Contrary to popular critical opinion, I think it is with Brennan
that we get the first genuinely unselfconscious Australian
poetry, and the first attempt at a human portrayal which has
more than a merely tribal significance. To read Brennan once
more is to encounter much that is clogged, and unworthy, and
even downright incompetent; but it is also to realize how
poignant his story is – of a tragic difficulty in art almost as
great as the difficulty which went so far to mar his life. What
the poetry reveals above all is the gulf between aspiration and
performance, the incongruity between the sweep of his imagination and the incomplete circling of his poetic talents. His view
of man's fate is majestic, but the poetic resources to his hand are

really less than adequate to that view. It may be, as Professor Randolph Hughes urges, that Australia was responsible for this anomaly — that Brennan did not find in the life around him material of a sufficiently malleable kind to localize his account of man's spiritual strivings. It is only in the more Irish-sounding rhythms, in 'The Wanderer' sequence, that his poetic soul seems to have found relief:

> I seem'd at home in some old dream of kingship:
> now it is clear grey day and the road is plain,
> I am the wanderer of many years
> who cannot tell if ever he was king
> or if ever kingdoms were: I know I am
> the wanderer of the ways of all the worlds,
> to whom the sunshine and the rain are one
> and one to stay or hasten, because he knows
> no ending of the way, no home, no goal,
> and phantom night and the grey day alike
> withhold the heart where all my dreams and days
> might faint in soft fire and delicious death:
> and saying this to myself as a simple thing
> I feel a peace fall in the heart of the winds
> and a clear dusk settle, somewhere, far in me.

This shows an elevated conception of eloquence which is unwelcome to most modern tastes; I may add that it is certainly not unwelcome to mine. It is personal, deeply, desperately so; yet it is also representative of the human condition in a way, and to a depth, which makes Lawson's attempt at representative statement appear no more than the shallow striking of an average. It presents us with the image of man in metaphysical action, and not simply with the details of his day. It is, in other words, really a poetry centred on man and pregnant with his image.

What one thinks of oneself is inevitably reflected in what one thinks of other men, and it is unerringly to be divined from the pictures one presents of others. Similarly, the aspects of oneself on which one is likely to dwell, and in which one is likely to find the materials for poetry, are intimately connected with one's heroes and imagined antagonists. Brennan saw man in the perspectives of Greek tragic literature; and he evidently estimated his own life as a subject for poetry in the light both of

that literature and of Christianity. Our later poets have tended
to take a view at once less noble and less consistent. Brennan
stands like a Colossus between the world of our first nationhood
and the world of our modern endeavours. After him come the
poets who rely for the philosophical vitality of their poetry
neither on Greek nobility nor on Christian. They are often either
vitalists or nationalists, or both. In the first case, they submit
man to the process of a sensuous romanticizing; in the second,
they submit him in his specifically Australian aspects to the
process of a congratulatory nationalist sentiment. And if I
dwell on these tendencies in modern Australian poetry, it is
because I believe them to have been in some ways dominant
ones, and dangerously inadequate ones.

We have Slessor and FitzGerald to thank for the specifically
modern development of poetry in this country; they have taught
our poetry how to deal with our history, and something of how
to see the land and its people. Yet there was a serpent in the
garden of these men's literary beginnings; it was the serpent of
vitalism as that creed was preached by the Lindsay group. Hugh
McCrae and the Lindsays influenced their view of what romance
and adventure are; and in their practical literary programme
McCrae and the Lindsays insisted mainly on their own brand
of the Four Freedoms, on anti-wowserism, in short; they kept
importing pans and satyrs, images of Diana and impossibly-
breasted women, to enliven an Australian landscape which
became transmuted by the unfamiliar contact. Contrary to
classical practice, in which one mythological figure was changed
into a tree, they changed gum trees into mythological figures. If
Slessor had not been possessed of such fine natural endowments,
they might have turned his head for ever; as it is, they went too
close to doing so.

It is unpleasant to carp at a poetic effort which has already
had its effect, but it is even more unpleasant to contemplate
the principal strains of that effort itself. The fleshy reliance on
the present moment and its joys may be a valuable corrective
to the kind of provincialism which we in Australia call
'wowserism': but it cannot be regarded as a particularly inspiring
programme for poetry. Hugh McCrae, that lively and often
lovely poet, gives us nevertheless a poetic universe in which man

is no more than a sum of erotic incidents. His manifesto may be gleaned from his own poem, 'Robin Hood':

> Now is the Venus-time of lusty Spring—
> Behold his tents, his toils on every holt!
> Gems on each twist and flowers unbuttoning,
> Jack-i'-the-hedge, hip-tree, and meadow colt.
>
> Now doth the partridge, (cock into his hen),
> Go tread . . . ash-grey with black, with white, with red . . .
> Plait-foot, the merry game all greenwood men
> Have done since Cupid first was bonneted.
>
> So shall I wear this shoe until it fit;
> Thou art my leman, lady-under-me:
> Laugh not or we are shent . . . no doubt of it . . .
> Where the mare squeals, *there* shall the stone-horse be.

Some of the phrasing here is apt and powerful; and it may be protested that McCrae's subject is a valid one for poetry. And so it is; but it must be held suspect when it and its attendant subjects come to set the tone for a nation's poetic development.

It is not eroticism which I am charging, but that vitalism of which eroticism is merely one of the inevitable expressions. Vitalism may be defined, very crudely, as the view which considers the primitive forces of life, amoral and irresistible, more important than the pattern of moral and aesthetic discriminations by which the adult human being lives. More than that; vitalism is anti-tragic, anti-spiritual, and ultimately anti-human. It cannot hold man central to the universe, because it holds biology central to man. In practice, it is a philosophy of the present moment. On the one hand, it can lead to despair; on the other, it can lead to McCrae's inane shout:

> I am the Lord, I am the Lord,
> I am the Lord of everything.

The idea which he expresses here is a mood, but it is a recurring one. There is nothing in it of the nobility of stoicism, certainly nothing of the greater nobility of Christianity. It is a restrictive ethos, leaving its possessors unready for too many of the inevitable human situations, and leaving their poetry incapable of assessing such situations as they do arise.

It is an important strain in our modern poetry; it dominates in a direct way the first books of both Slessor and FitzGerald. In a more indirect way, it has heavily influenced the poetry of Douglas Stewart and Kenneth MacKenzie, the poetry and prose of Eve Langley, even the work of Judith Wright and Brian Vrepont. Norman Lindsay is really its spiritual father. He reveals as much in his visual art, in his novels, and in the emphasis which his criticism places on earthiness and on the irreducibility of passion. It is true that Lindsay also stresses the duty of a poet to face up to the realities of his life. And in this I support him wholeheartedly; poetry has no use for the strategies, whether of convention or of overcharged emotion, by which man tries to escape himself and his fleshed circumstances. But to transcend is not the same thing as to escape; the choice is not between Shelley and Browning (or, at least, Lindsay's conception of Browning); a man may live at once in the flesh and in the spirit. I believe that Lindsay himself dangerously misconceives (and in misconceiving, underrates) what *are* the realities of human life. In so doing, he does not free, but rather limits, the subject-matter of poetry.

I dwell at such length on these points because, as they have been often presented, they have influenced all the poets I have mentioned, and many others besides. This pagan and mysta-gogical vitalism has become a view both of human action and of the imagination; it has produced poetry of an occa-sional excitement or loveliness, in Stewart's *The Dosser in Springtime*, McCrae's *Satyrs and Sunlight*, and MacKenzie's *The Moonlit Doorway*; but on the whole it is a limited and limiting view; it inhibits the intellect and the moral imagination, substituting for them sensation and romantic fancy which (as Coleridge rightly insists) are by no means the same things as their more imperative cousins.

It is a poetry which relies too exclusively on bodily sensation, and on the emotional fantasies which such a reliance is apt to breed. Eve Langley, herself an unimportant writer, is a good example of such a tendency carried to its extreme; so are Norman Lindsay's preoccupation with the buttock as a symbol of power, and the roistering tavern scenes in the early poetry of Kenneth Slessor. And it is precisely this strain which is so largely responsible for the intellectual retardation of our poetry. These men, or at least some of them, scorn intellectual values; and, as they rely on too limited a range of personal experience, so do they rely on too narrow a resource of tradition. Despite a superficial resemblance, Villon and Rabelais and Burns have little to do with the spirit of our local Pan-worshippers; these latter live on the margins of a world which is dominated by the values of the *Heptameron, The Yellow Book,* and Balzac's great aberration, the *Droll Stories.* Their work may be summed up as an aesthetic and erotic vitalism given a larrikin flavour.

Nor is it a particularly passionate poetry. It is really a poetry of bravado; all cock-crow, and little loving. What energy comes finally to dwell in it as a result of the distillation of poetry is largely verbal. In other words, it is an art of naïve verbosity. And I should say that it is part of FitzGerald's success as a poet that he should so consistently have developed away from its influence, and found a personal creative answer to it.

The other great strain which has in my opinion retarded the growth of our poetry to full maturity is that of nationalism. But as soon as this word is used, ambiguities begin to creep in; for nationalism has as many disguises as the director of a puppet-show. The focal-point of our modern nationalism is, of course, the Jindyworobak movement in which, when the verse is not merely one of nature description, we find a propaganda at once clamorous and quasi-mystical. But, at the same time, the *Bulletin, Overland,* and *Southerly* seem to be strong-points of a nationalism which is perhaps less exclusive and less insistent.

It seems to me that this late growth is an attempt to answer, whether directly or otherwise, a certain spontaneous movement in our poetry. As the nation's experience widened, with the access of war and the growth of its city-life, so did the subject-matter of poetry. Maurice and Gellert and Brennan widened it, each in his own way. And after them, as I have said, there came a conscious though misguided attempt to de-provincialize poetry, in the magazine *Vision,* and in the early work of Slessor and FitzGerald. But nationalism remained strong, and it has since become stronger, to the point of being a pervasive influence.

It works through an insistence on a national subject-matter and a natural human type; and since it cannot make good its claims by taking Australian men as the majority of them in fact live, it has had to become a poetry of the outback. The insistence on outback scenes and perspectives is quite alarming in the extent to which it dominates our poetic thinking. So is the insistence on national stereotypes, on the idea that Australian man can be comprised within the limits of a formula. This formula, this stereotype, has generally been that of the bushman, the man acquainted with the inner life of the country, and living to its rhythms. Australian man is tough, independent, matey, and possessed of the secrets of the world; so Ray Mathew writes of the Happy Farmer:

> Here is the young farmer: he isn't clever,
> isn't handsome; he speaks with a drawl.
> But he is tall, and strong, and holds himself
> consciously: is proud and laughing about the crop
> he's planted, smiling a little and boasting
> when the wheat is green with promise. His wife
> isn't pretty. But she's young, and working, and she does,
> and they are married. . . . The wheat that's green
> for him is green for her, and proud.

This is a curious conception of the human possibilities of poetry. Mathew's manner, the laconic, stoical drawl, is deliberately attuned to what he considers the universal nature of the farmer's appeal. So, at any rate, Mathew. And so Douglas Stewart, in an unaccustomed relapse into nativism, reduces the man on the land further towards his mystical source and type, the aboriginal stockman:

> Oh he was dark as the gibber stones
> And took things just as easy
> And a white smile danced on his purple lips
> Like an everlasting daisy.
>
> The horses strayed on the saltbush plain
> And he went galloping after,
> The green shirt flew through the coolibah trees
> Like budgerigars to water.

And then what need had he to sigh
For old men under the gibbers
When he was free as the winds that blow
Along the old dry rivers?

It is rollicking enough; it is neither halting nor inane; Douglas Stewart cannot help being a poet whenever he writes. Others, however, are not so fortunately endowed. The Jindyworobaks are, on the whole, not greatly talented men; and this fact gives their silliness a much greater play, even a greater solemnity. I do not want to deal here with the members of this movement; they have been the occasion for enough comment already, and perhaps of enough misrepresentation. It is only their thorough-going maintenance of their own doctrines which has made them anything of a force at all. Where the Communist poets choose national subjects, national stereotypes, even allegedly 'national' verse-forms in the ballad and ballad-lyric, for a political reason, the Jindyworobaks do so for a reason which seems religious rather than political. And this quasi-religious intention colours all the local detail of their verse. How far it goes in doctrinaire thoroughness may be seen in a remark made by Rex Ingamells,[1] – a remark which I personally find astonishingly naïve and reactionary. In suggesting that even the apt presentation of an Australian scene is not properly indigenous if it is shown as inhabited by a white settlement, he says:

> What may be called 'colonial' or 'settlement' description of our outback was effectively achieved in poetry long before the essential problem of presenting the purely indigenous scene was properly realized . . . early settlers altered the landscape, as best they could, in ways to suit themselves . . .

I have been most selective in quoting from this passage, in order to bring out its central suggestion that the land is somehow more 'poetic', more significant, when it is seen deprived of any white life, which is essentially alien to it.

Vitalism and nationalism have been, therefore, the retarding forces on our poetry. The first of these would substitute the reign of impulse and sensation for that of any kind of realism –

---

[1] *The Age* Literary Supplement, 26 March 1955.

whether sensuous, spiritual, intellectual, or social. The second of them would, in various ways, hold our poetry back to the emotional atmosphere and the literary forms of the nineties of last century. It is true that there are problems for Australian poetry, and that these two tendencies represent two separate attempts to meet those problems. One of the problems is that our literary sensibility tends to be European, that our beliefs and attitudes are part of the Western tradition and have always found their dominant symbols in Western society, but that we ourselves live geographically in Asia, and moreover in an immediate physical environment which is quite distinctive, with something of the primitive about it. That is one problem, and our poets have been, at least implicitly, aware of it. The nationalists have reacted to its challenge by trying to eliminate the European sensibility, and to substitute other emotional attitudes and beliefs for those which underlie it. The vitalists have reacted by scanting the question of ideas, and by rendering Australia into the material for a fanciful romanticism which has no roots in any locality at all. Our best poets, however, have attempted, whether consciously or not, to fuse the two traditions; it is in the resulting struggle that our poetry has come to attain whatever degree of maturity it now possesses.

It is a definite attempt to do what has never been successfully done before, to achieve a mutual adjustment of the objective and subjective worlds – the world of Australian landscape and manners with the world of European morality, and art, and spiritual values. I cannot see any other lines on which our poetry can continue to grow. Judith Wright speaks openly of her intention to be part of such a growth:

> Your trees, the homesick and the swarthy native,
> blow all one way to me, this southern weather
> that smells of early snow:
> 　　　　　And I remember
> the house closed in with sycamore and chestnut
> fighting the foreign wind.
> Here I will stay, she said; be done with the black north,
> the harsh horizon rimmed with drought. –
> Planted the island there and drew it round her.
> Therefore I find in me the double tree.

The two fusing forces are here symbolized in the growth of two kinds of tree together – the kindly English and the fierce Australian. James McAuley speaks of a different aspect of the same struggle, but with a very similar intention:

> And I am fitted to that land as the soul is to the body,
> I know its contractions, waste, and sprawling indolence;
> They are in me and its triumphs are my own,
> Hard-won in the thin and bitter years without pretence.
>
> Beauty is order and good chance in the artesian heart
> And does not wholly fail, though we impede;
> Though the reluctant and uneasy land resent
> The gush of waters, the lean plough, the fretful seed.

It is an awareness (at least a stumbling and partial one) of these issues which has helped to give such relative vitality to much of our contemporary poetry. In the best work of Slessor and FitzGerald, we find the land largely assimilated as landscape, and the life of the people quite well assumed to the poetic imagination. They now *see* Australia, where the poets up to O'Dowd merely *conceived* it. The land was coming, because of its very immediacy, to be seen as an historical reality, a definite entity with a definite historical place, very different from the apocalyptic but unbelievable land of O'Dowd's fancy. One of the themes in the best work of these two (as in that of younger poets like Francis Webb and Douglas Stewart) was discovery, the discovery of the land as a total presence. We do not find this theme as it were unalloyed, but we do find it, and in a prominent position. It was a valuable way of insisting on the historical fact of Australia, where earlier poets had seen only the social fact. It was a way, too, of linking up the land as a whole with certain of the ideas and aspirations of Europe since the fifteenth century, the Europe of the explorers. This whole strain has close affinities with poetic nationalism, but it is at once more sophisticated and more firmly centred on the human being than that precarious creed. It is also more dramatic, as Slessor shows:

> How many mariners had made that choice
> Paused on the brink of mystery! 'Choose now!'
> The winds roared, blowing home, blowing home,
> Over the Coral Sea. 'Choose now!' the trades

Cried once to Tasman, throwing him for choice
Their teeth or shoulders, and the Dutchman chose
The wind's way, turning north. 'Choose, Bougainville!'
The wind cried once, and Bougainville had heard
The voice of God, calling him prudently
Out of a dead lee shore, and chose the north,
The wind's way. So, too, Cook made choice,
Over the brink, into the devil's mouth,
With four months' food, and sailors wild with dreams
Of English beer, the smoking barns of home.
So Cook made choice, so Cook sailed westabout,
So men write poems in Australia.

Here is a view of man whose urge to discovery (or is it merely self-realization?) drives him into battle with the elements; but it is a meaningful struggle, made meaningful by the courage implicit in its motives and by the civilization explicit in its achievements. It seems solitary and asocial, and so in a way it is; yet it points towards social values. It is an openly, even defiantly eloquent poetry, and it implies a dramatic view of man; adventure is its keynote, and the constant cry of adventure makes it seem a little crude, a little over-insistent. Yet it, or something like it, was necessary for the healthy growth of our poetry; it is not lachrymose, not conventional, not static in its posing of man against his fate. It is a much more satisfying conception than any which the various outback schools have managed to foist on our editors as 'The Australian Tradition'. And if the struggles which it portrays have no tragic element, do not touch heaven or hell, are too easily resolved by action, they are nevertheless struggles symbolic of man's role in the world.

It is the first genuinely poetic attempt to construct a myth of Australia which is rooted in our actual historical condition. Since the appearance of Slessor's first book, the struggle of our poetry towards spiritual maturity has at every phase involved such a myth-making activity. And if the myths contradict one another, if their characteristic images will not sort the one with another, it is no great matter. The adventure poems of Slessor and Fitz-Gerald (as of their lineal descendants) show man as an adventurer, but in his own land, his own imaginative climate; they exhibit a view of man which is consequently of a deeply personal kind as well as concerned with objective general statements.

Most of the other myth-making activities are important not as poetry but as a literary politics. You do not produce a national poetry from the febrile, the obscurantist, and the inane. And the best of our younger poets, concerned with the personal depths of poetry, have developed apart from such activities. They have taken up the challenge implicit in the experiments of Slessor and FitzGerald, and they have given greater spiritual gravity to their materials. In their work, we find a deepening of sensibility to the point where the land is conceived and imagined in terms which are at once spiritual, moral, sensory, and directed to the drama of human existence. In Judith Wright, this movement leads to a kind of pantheistic identification of man and his natural environment. In McAuley, it leads to a vision of society and of the artist representing society. In Rosemary Dobson, it touches the delicate webbing of human perceptions. In John Thompson, it is first socially conscious, and then gustily ironic. In A. D. Hope, it moves securely into the basic paradox of man, balanced as he is between beast and angel. In Francis Webb, it strives desperately to wed hard thought to a myriad powerful impressions. We get, as we have never got before, a poetry of which man is the effective and affective centre – man as the poet lives and represents him; and we get with it a greater variety of moods and talents than we have had at any one time before.

For the best of the younger poets are less concerned with striking attitudes than with finding out the deepest truths about themselves and their destinies. There has been, in fact, a continuation and deepening of the theme of discovery in the work of Webb, McAuley, Hope, Judith Wright, and Douglas Stewart. None of them is, in any obvious or insistent way, Australian; but each of them has in his own individual way begun to bring together into a satisfying synthesis the objective and the subjective, the true and the emotionally stimulating, European culture and Australian fact.

We have reached the point in our cultural development where it becomes both possible and imperative for the poet to search out the spiritual realities behind the social and historical ones,

to speak of misery and of joy alike as spiritual things, having
an intimate connection with our daily life, yet having at the
same time an archetypal quality, and fitting even into the
dimensions of heaven and hell.

The keynote of the best recent poetry is not discovery of the
land, but adjustment to it. I am not suggesting for a moment
that McAuley and Judith Wright, to name only two, have
abandoned the struggle to seek out general spiritual truths. On
the contrary, they have taken up this struggle at a deeper level
and with a more strenuous will than any of their predecessors
except Brennan. But the essence of their struggle is the attempt
to find out themselves and their deepest values in relation to a
land of which, factually, they are already sufficiently aware. It
is self-discovery as well as world-discovery.

And if they ask themselves the perennial questions about
man and his destiny, they ask them generally through the
medium of images native to Australia (many of them great
primal images that come to have the stature of recurrent
symbols) and even in the despised Australian accent. So
Elizabeth Riddell chants out, in a song which might almost be
considered an ironic answer to Douglas Stewart's 'Sombrero':

> As I went out to walk
> Beside the river flowing
> I saw what I'd not hoped to see:
> A black man washing a white horse.
> That's how the world was going.
>
> He washed the horse's tail
> And plaited it with yellow,
> The wild west show had come to town,
> That's how I saw the high white horse
> And the brave black fellow . . .
>
> I never hope to see again
> A white horse decked in yellow,
> The hawks, the horse, the river in flood,
> The cowboy's eyes of bitter blue
> Or the brave black fellow.

But it is difficult to particularize, to choose names and shift
categories, to be always separating point from point. The in-

creasing humanity, the increasing variety, which our poetry
has achieved over the past ten years are as they should be. We
are still to some extent lacking in thought, still lacking in fiery
and decisive images of man, still scared of the final spiritual
dimensions and of the interior experiments necessary to reveal
them. We are still not quite modern, as other literatures understand modernity. Yet we are on our way to being mature. And
as in an individual, so in a society; the maturity of poetic
expression depends on the terms which it has developed to help
in the elucidation and exalted judgment of man's common
experience. This applies, I believe, even when the poet seems to
live a life utterly remote, both in its quality and in its preoccupations, from the life of his fellows.

It may be that we have really been developing such terms
here in Australia. The results are not evident, but the tendencies
are. As I have said elsewhere, there have been forces contributing
to, there have been other forces militating against, the development of a rich and humanist convention in our poetry. This
essay, after all, is the record of thirty years' confused struggle
to establish such a convention. Some of the attempts have been
directed to making this convention universal, to adapting it
(no matter how strong its local roots) to the manners, as well as
the spirit, of contemporary European work. And it is worth
noting that the arguments for a local literature, a literature
strongly rooted in a local place and atmosphere, are not at all
the same as the arguments for a nationalist bias and stereotype.
To give to an idea a local habitation and a name is not to
nationalize it, as though it were a bank or a species of native
fauna. It is the error of the anti-Europeans to pretend that such
a distinction between localism and nationalism does not exist;
it is their folly to have attempted to take short-cuts towards the
gaining of a maturity which only a different and more interior
dedication is capable of earning. European values can live in
Australian forms; and if we seek further, we find that they are
not in any exclusive sense European at all, but universal, and
merely exemplified most finely in the cultures of Europe.
Nationalism seems to me a concept as restrictive in poetry as
it is in international politics. It tries to be at once exclusive and
typical; it leads to the sanctification of force through a coerced

majority; it deals not with men but with bloodless abstractions which demand· human blood if they are ever to have the appearance of life.

It is tremendously important, now of all times, to ask the right questions. Australianness is certainly no longer our dominant literary issue, if indeed it ever was. And when it is raised as the issue, by Rex Ingamells and others, it is often raised on the wrong level, in such a way as to presuppose an irrelevant answer. But it is not the issue. The issue is one of spiritual development, of the social and cultural manners which will express that development, and of the poetic forms in which to contain and advance it.

In England thirty years ago, Eliot and Pound were seeking, among other goals, a security of manners, literary as well as moral. They sought at once a pattern of life truly expressive of creative values, and a pattern of poetry adequate to its reflection. Since that day, English poetry has sought even more desperately for it. But such a search has (paradoxically enough) proved not nearly so important in Australian poetry, with its greater signs of stability and growth. Eternity for Australians is not enshrined in buildings, cultural habits, social institutions, but in nature, in the land herself. And so, progress for us has not so far existed in the mind or in the expanding passionate heart, but in material things. It is obvious to every eye that we are not disintegrating, but growing; and from this very fact we deduce a pattern of manners into which our lives will fit easily enough. Will fit, that is, unless we are somehow moved to think deeply and passionately on the substance of those very lives; for the eye is not the sole judge, does not possess the only charter of efficiency. The view I have just been expressing is superficial and silly, of course, but it is held, it is Australian; more than that, it is lived – and that is the greatest compliment which men can pay to their beliefs.

No doubt there is in Australia, as there is everywhere, a radical confusion of values; but Australian man is not conscious of it. We do not discern it in our everyday lives, or even in our politics, where it exists most clamorously. And unless we find some way of discerning it, our poetry cannot come fully to maturity; for we will lack manners based on a sufficiently grave and spiritual awareness.

As I have said earlier, to look over the array of Australian poetry on the bookshelves is to be conscious of an imaginative world which is itself simply not aware of certain dimensions of experience. We seem to live in history in a minor way – as second-class citizens of her territory. Our poetry gives little hint of the metaphysical vision of the European or Asian past; nor does it give much hint of the spiritual convulsions which are at the moment agonizing every society and burning beneath the surface of our own. And if our steady growth in sureness and variety has been the measure of our relative success, this lack of tragic awareness is the measure of our relative failure.

Thirty Years of Technique

I MUST APOLOGIZE for using (or seeming to use) my very title to beg the question which this essay is designed to explore. The word 'technique' has always seemed to me an ugly and inexpressive one; most of my waking life I despise and detest both the word itself and the conception of poetry which is all too often implied in its use. But it seems there are no other words to express one whole aspect of poetic practice. There are paraphrases, but they are not quite the same thing; and one cannot ask one's title, limping as it is, to bear the additional burden of its own paraphrase.

The 'thirty years' refers, of course, to the last thirty years of Australian poetry – to the development within it of a recognizably 'modern' strain and emphasis. And if the word 'technique' may displease some people, others may be even more disquieted by the suggestion that this curious term can be given a placing at once geographical and temporal, that we can speak of a technique springing up in Australia over a number of decades which may be enumerated and named. Someone may say that, if technique means anything at all, it surely signifies a use of words which is personal, and cannot be communal; that it cannot, in itself, be a tradition, a readily transferable ticket or currency, a commodity available for export from the individual poet to his fellows, or vice versa.

Others may insist that, even if all this were possible, we should still be unjustified in thinking of it in isolation, in considering such a currency apart from the context, either of social habits or of a body of poetry, which gives it a social value and meaning. And I agree: it is risky to consider it as though in isolation. Consequently, I have been careful to write first on the image of man in Australian poetry, in the hope of providing a context which will give some effect to my present remarks. Yet there are modes of thought and feeling, both in society and in the individual poet, modes which are reflected in a verbal convention, a characteristic use of poetic form; we may, with due precaution, examine this convention and characteristic use, knowing that we strike beneath it to a poetic substance.

In writing these notes, therefore, I use my central term in the sense of 'an attitude to, and use of, poetic form and elements'; and I shall attempt to comment not only on what is common to the modern Australian poets, but also on what is changing and varied in their work. In doing so, I shall be noting an effect, without much reference to the social occasions of which it is the by-product, and with almost none at all to the emotional drives of its individual authors.

It is necessary, in dealing with the development of Australian poetry over the past thirty years, to insist that the development has been, in the broadest sense and to the deepest degree, technical. Our poets have achieved an added hardness, both in imagery and in the outline of their poems – a new complexity and concreteness. They have begun to use varied and relaxed rhythms, to decline any longer to compose either in the 'sequence of the metronome' or in that of a purely lyrical mode; and they have reinforced their rhythmic changes by the discreet use of colloquial touches. They have achieved certain modulations of the lyrical note by making their work more dramatic or more intellectual. And, above all, they have come slowly but surely to the use of poetic forms not to announce conclusions nor to present moods persuasively, but to help explore the questions which incite them to poetry.

I have said 'they'; and such a series of generalizations may seem to express no more than the usual paranoia of the literary critic; yet generalizations are necessary if one is to pose any case at all. The changes which I have outlined so briefly are of course among the changes to which modern poetry has in every country committed itself. As they occur in Australia, however, they have by no means exhausted the range of innovations which we find in English and American poetry over a comparable period. Australian poetry is still far more muted and stable, far less experimental, than the work of the British or Americans. More than that, it presents an entirely different literary climate; it has followed the poetry of the older countries neither in the range of its developments nor in their sequence; it insists on different qualities and on different forms in which to express them. It has certainly been influenced by overseas developments; but it has not been determined by them. It is, as every local poetry should be, *sui generis*, retaining and strengthening something of its own.

Not everyone will agree. Mr James Devaney will not; nor, it seems, will Professor R. G. Howarth. These two critics are startlingly different in their emphases, as in the literary values which they espouse; the one represents the extreme Right of criticism, the other a moderate but doctrinaire Left. Yet they seem to be agreed on the proposition that modern Australian poetry has followed English poetry in its growth, and has come to share its values; for Mr Devaney, the change is 'modernist' and bad; for Professor Howarth, it varies between 'modern' and 'modernist' but is, in any case, good.

Mr Devaney puts his essential case in one paragraph, before extending it to the length of a book :

> Here, then, was modernism in verse, the new blueprint for poetry. It was really a private method for poetry, T. S. Eliot's pasticcio selected from his various sources and synthesized into a unity which was his own. The main components were its emphasis upon the contemporary and the new, upon satiric wit, obscurity, a prose diction; its repudiation of the personal, the romantic, the traditional; its scorn of beauty, emotion, the abstract, the inspirational.[1]

This author writes with considerable party-spirit, strengthened by his very real puzzlement at what has actually been happening in modern poetry, both here and in England. And if his brief account were a true one, he would have every right, indeed, he would have a positive duty, to be puzzled and resentful. But it is not a true account, and his feelings seem as irrelevant as they are ineffectual. He has confused the pretensions of poetasters with the temporary experimental zeal of poets; and he has confused the tangled web of English poetry, its changes of emphasis and allegiance, with the calmer development of poetry in Australia. He is right in commenting that a love of newness and of obscurity, a repudiation of the personal and the traditional, are not positive poetic values at all; but he has apparently failed to learn that such cleavages, such repudiations, are neither advocated nor practised by good modern poets anywhere; least of all are they generally advocated or practised in Australia.

[1] *Poetry in Our Time* (M.U.P., 1952), p. 18.

Mr Devaney does not really know what changes are involved in the kind of poetry which he calls modernist; Professor Howarth knows a great deal about them. Where Mr Devaney rejects the modern experiments, *he* accepts them with whole-hearted gratitude and sympathy:

> Of the modernists in Australia, some – especially Chris. Brennan, Kenneth Slessor, Robert D. FitzGerald, T. Inglis Moore (a social critic, like Auden and his group), Paul Grano, John Manifold, Douglas Stewart, A. D. Hope (a satirist), John Thompson, David Campbell, and James McAuley – rank with the English and American poets . . .[2]

and, as he goes on to imply, run parallel to those English and American modernists with whom they share a common ranking. Professor Howarth is immensely more knowledgeable and sophisticated than Mr Devaney, but his booklet is nevertheless a rather queer treatise. It is true that it does not pretend to give a complete account of a movement, but merely to act as a handbook of new technical uses and terms; it has a most exhaustive, and rather frightening, table of technical revivals and innovations; yet it presupposes much of what Mr Devaney also presupposes about the nature of our modern poetry. Despite his insistence that the modern poet is attempting to 'interpret, in its proper terms, his own time', he consistently analyses the elements of modern experiment as though they had a purely literary source and value, as though they were merely technical in the narrow sense of that word. And he has no hesitation in predicating of Australian poets the same conscious manipulation of poetic devices that he predicates of the English poets. For him, it is all the one movement, and it contains the same set of usable elements.

I cannot help finding his analysis in many respects queer and question-begging, although it is certainly thorough and thoughtful. Two or three of the Australians whose names he includes are not significant poets at all; and the majority of the others cannot be regarded as modernists in the sense in which Auden and Spender, Eliot and Dylan Thomas can be regarded as modernists. It is interesting that his main exemplar in Australian

[2] *Notes on Modern Poetic Technique, English and Australian* (Angus & Robertson, Sydney, 1949), pp. 6-7.

poetry is Kenneth Slessor; yet it cannot possibly be claimed of
Slessor that he 'interprets his own time' in anything like the
same sense, or with anything like the same poetic means, as does
Auden or Eliot.

The fallacy (if there is one in Professor Howarth's booklet)
arises from his tendency to think of the elements of poetry as
completely malleable, as absolutely disposable in any context
according to the conscious decision of the poet; and he sees them
as justified not so much by their inner integrity as by their
effectiveness in stimulating certain surface effects. I cannot help
rejecting this view of things. Any poetic 'mode' is suspect according to how much it claims to achieve. One cannot have a
revolution in poetic diction without being prepared to take the
consequences, to follow its implications. And, insofar as the
modern movement, either here or abroad, has been of positive
poetic value, it is not merely a question of 'diction' in the
narrow sense; it is a question of all the inter-relating parts and
elements of language as a poet finds them necessary to the
pressure of his inspiration. Speech-habits in poetry, which is all
that the word 'diction' means, do not comprise only vocabulary
and characteristic figures of speech, but also tone, pitch, habits
of compressed and allusive language, all the changes which the
use of metre and the stresses of that much-scanted word 'inspiration' enjoin on the poet. Looked at from this aspect, diction
or technique is the whole pattern of the word-uses which the
habitus of poetry entails. It is therefore a personal thing, part
of the very being and interior presence of the poet; and we may
detect a common diction only where there is an undue amount
of imitation, or where a number of poets, being subject to much
the same exterior influences, share much the same attitude to
life and poetry, and reflect their common attitude in a common
habit of speech. Even so, there will be wide variations from poet
to poet; for, no matter what influences may be shared, the interior springs of poetry are always personal and profound.
These are deductions which Wordsworth in his evangelical
fervour for the common language of men failed adequately to
draw, and which Coleridge used in correcting him on this very
part of his aesthetic theory.

Genuine poetic movements, therefore, do not arise from an

attitude to poetry alone, from the simple desire to create or to restore a literary mode; they arise from poetry's reaction to certain external pressures; and they always involve an intense degree of self-awareness on the part of a number of poets who are concerned about their own vocations. This is as true of modern poetry as it is of Romanticism. It was an awareness of certain pressing problems in society which led to English modernism; and the relatively unmodern nature of Australian poetry is obviously due to the fact that there has been among our poets no comparable awareness.

It would be a mistake to conclude that modern poetry sprang fully-armed from Eliot's desire to foist on the world a new and paradoxical kind of academicism, or from Pound's obsession with 'making it new'. Professor Howarth, of course, does not suggest any such conclusion; Mr Devaney seems to have pinned his whole argument to it.

Eliot and Pound have certainly been responsible for the introduction into the English tradition of certain ideas which have, it is true, become obligatory in certain circles. They introduced a new attitude to poetry as a recorder of life, to poetic subjects, and to poetic technique.

In the first place, they saw that Georgian poetry, and the whole tendency in English verse which derived from the followers of Tennyson, were little more than a series of evasions. The poet was using the habit of verse-composition to evade the central problems of his life; he recorded neither the movements of society as it really was, nor the movements of his interior life as it really was; under the delicate dispensations of Georgian and Tennysonian verse, the art of poetry was not so much wrong as irrelevant; poetry had become a game played in cap and bells around a maypole on a country green. There was no propagandist intention in Eliot's awareness of all this; there was simply a determination to recover the lost power of poetry, by recovering the intense awareness of reality on which that power was based. And so poetry was to become a means of evaluating life in the very act of recording it.

Something similar happened in Australia, though it was not the product of such an intense awareness, and it was not accompanied by such a conscious determination. The beginnings of modernism in England carried their own rationale; its beginnings in Australia did not. The introduction of a new intention into Australian poetry may be dated about the early twenties of this century, about the date of the publication of Eliot's 'The Waste Land'. But where 'The Waste Land' attempts a most vivid comparative evaluation of a whole society, the writers associated with the short-lived magazine, *Vision*, were interested only in the recovery of a primitive vitality of spirit. The two tendencies have almost nothing in common, even if we allow that they were both, in their different ways, the products of post-war *malaise*. One has only to look at the poetry which Slessor and Jack Lindsay were producing at this time, and the point becomes clear; such verse was by no means the reflection and evaluation of Australian society, or, indeed, of any other; it was a private, adolescent fantasy, fabulous and over-excited. I cannot even suggest whence their desire for a more vital poetry was derived; certainly, it was not derived from any stable and adult awareness of a deprivation in society.

The second thing which the English modernists brought into poetry, besides a new sense of its social relevance, was a new attitude to poetic subjects. I am not referring to the demand that sordid subjects be used, or that 'unpoetic' words, like 'pylons' and 'nylons', 'gantry' and 'protoplasm', should become the staple of a new diction. I am referring to something far more fundamental to the social intentions of the experimenters. Eliot and Pound, and the intolerable Sitwells, were determined to investigate, and to express in the very form of their poetry, the crisis of a civilization; this obviously could not be done without the use of certain areas of experience which poetry had for decades neglected to use, and the introduction of certain new attitudes and tones. Accordingly, paradox and irony became usual in poetry even in cases where the apparent subject was of a quite 'traditional' kind. At the same time, since these poets were concerned with an interior crisis of human thought and feeling, they were anxious to place modern man within the context of his own historical past. So there was an access of richness in poetic texture, of complexity of tone, of a wide range of reference and allusion.

There was, in addition, a tendency not only to look askance at present-day society, but also to cast a nostalgic eye over the surface detail of societies of the past. A static, undramatic view of man tended to develop, and in its turn to produce a certain static quality in imagery and rhythm; yet, all the while, man was the focus of the poet's attention — man not perhaps in his full presence and interiority, but man as a social function, man as an external state. Eliot and Pound had taken society's estimate of man in order to turn it back with trenchant irony on society itself:

> The silent man in mocha brown
> Sprawls at the window-sill and gapes;
> The waiter brings in oranges
> Bananas figs and hothouse grapes;
>
> The silent vertebrate in brown
> Contracts and concentrates, withdraws;
> Rachel *née* Rabinovitch
> Tears at the grapes with murderous paws;
>
> She and the lady in the cape
> Are suspect, thought to be in league;
> Therefore the man with heavy eyes
> Declines the gambit, shows fatigue,
>
> Leaves the room and reappears
> Outside the window, leaning in,
> Branches of wistaria
> Circumscribe a golden grin;
>
> The host with someone indistinct
> Converses at the door apart,
> The nightingales are singing near
> The Convent of the Sacred Heart,
>
> And sang within the bloody wood
> When Agamemnon cried aloud,
> And let their liquid siftings fall
> To stain the stiff dishonoured shroud.

No matter what else one may say of it, this was an extremely sophisticated poetry, in which every stanza, every juxtaposition of images or movements, reflects the ambiguity of man's action in the world as the poet sees it. For years, Australian poetry did not reflect such an ambiguity; and it has never learnt to do so with anything approaching Eliot's sophistication and complete awareness. The reason obviously is that we in Australia have never been moved to feel such an ambiguity at all. I have said that our poetry which was contemporary with 'The Waste Land' proved to be nearly opposite in spirit to Eliot's poem. And it was not merely a question of the inevitable time-lag between the beginning of an idea in England and its eventual appearance in Australia. Many of the modernist ideas have never influenced our poetry. Just at the time when we might have expected the influence of Eliot's view of subject-matter to have become influential among our poets, in the mid-thirties, we find, in fact, our leading poets, FitzGerald and Slessor, moving in quite a different direction. In the place of a poetry which attempts to realize the full ambiguity of man's place in history, we have a poetry of relatively simple aspiration and aims. In place of Pound's translations from the Chinese and the Provençal, we have a widespread and often dramatically effective reliance on themes of discovery and exploration, conquest and adventure. In place of the minutiae which cluttered the life of Eliot's sentimental friend in 'Portrait of a Lady', we have the great sweep of the Spanish and Portuguese and Dutch explorers. In place of the growing cosmopolitanism of English poetry, we have the various shapes of Australian nationalism, whether explicit or concealed, casual or doctrinaire. It is simply a different imaginative world from that plotted by Eliot, and later by Auden and MacNeice. In the best Australian poetry of the thirties, man is viewed as an animal who seeks not primarily a social status and stability, but the conquest of time and space. As late as 1945, this was a strain evident in the work of McAuley, Douglas Stewart, and FitzGerald:

> But man's essence
> is not nobility, it is man, unrest,
> a rushing of wind, distance: distance which is
> in the heart as much as in worn shoes – a carpet
> unrolled over the world as we unroll one
> over these earthen tiles when there is music
> and little Micaela dancing. Man is these things;
> and life's like a wave breaking – not good or ill,
> or right or wrong, but action and pressing forward;

a thing tested in the heart, which hears and answers;
as when we have men, near-naked and ill-armed,
thirteen, half-starved, setting out to conquer kingdoms.

It is true that there is often in the 'exploration' poems of contemporary Australian poets a note of nostalgia for a past when
exploration was possible, in a way in which it is not possible
today. But there is also a realization that a poetic treatment of
the early explorers is valuable only if we can use them as symbols
and examples relevant to our own situation in the modern
world. In this sense, our poetry is modern, is concerned with
the fate of man here and now. But it is concerned with that fate
less openly, less directly, than Eliot and Auden; and it is concerned not so much with man's place in society as with his place
in the context of nature. It is concerned to establish the possibility of human action rather than the reality of certain human
states. And in all this, the influence of the leading English
modernists is not at all discernible.

One may say that our poets are akin to the English in that
they are now prepared to recognize the poetic propriety of a
larger range of subjects than most of the earlier poets did. This
is true; but they do not seem to want to take much advantage
of their newly developed liberality. Where they treat 'contemporary subjects', (and I am not sure that one is entitled to speak
in these terms), they treat them with vastly different precon-
ceptions from those which the English poets use.

The third great innovation made by the English poets was
an innovation in poetic technique, in the very handling of words.
The climate of English poetry in the twenties of this century
is truly an astonishing one to contemplate in retrospect. Free
verse, sometimes with a scarcely discernible iambic base, sometimes so closely allied to prose that its effectiveness depended
on its being distributed in curious patterns on the printed page,
became a quite normal poetic form; it became almost the
requisite way of expressing the disillusionment and the frag-
mentation of thought which many people hold to be typical of
our age. In place of a poetry of statement, of balanced and
persuasive rhythm, we had a new tradition of allusion, of
abruptly variant rhythms, of image replacing statement instead
of consolidating it. We were given a new attitude to symbolism,

and an emphasis on what Eliot pertinently named 'the objective correlative' – a device for releasing emotion and at the same time disguising it.

Now, free verse has had in England its period of dubious glory, and there is a general return to a different use of poetic forms. There is no need in Australia for such a re-adjustment, for there has not been the general addiction to free verse which would make a re-adjustment necessary. The best of the Australian poets over the past thirty years have been somewhat reserved in their formal experiments. What seems, from one point of view, a lack of enterprise or even a failure of creative nerve, is actually determined by the conception of poetry to which these poets adhere. We may find, in Judith Wright, or McAuley, or Francis Webb, examples of a fairly free use of poetic form; but it is not general in their work, or in the work of our other good poets; on the contrary, there is a marked preference for relatively traditional forms, even where these are employed with a relative liberality. And the reason is that our poetry has never become detached from certain recurrent human situations, from the obviously *human*, and so has never ceased to be a poetry of statement as well as of allusion. In a poetry where statement is as important as imagery, the use of poetic form, except in extraordinary cases, will tend to be rather a traditional one. Australian poets have, of course, experimented; but whereas Fitz-Gerald's later work brings us a new conception of dramatic poetry, it does so in forms which are in themselves close to a traditional conception. The experiments are in an approach to statement rather than in form.

If the use of completely new forms has been far from general, so has the desire to revive old, quaint forms – either out of an antiquarian interest or from a sense of irony. There is no parallel in our poetry for MacNeice's 'Eclogues', for the verse epistles of the thirties, or for the Sestina. The kind of complexity of mind which wrily chooses such outmoded forms for its expression is not characteristic here. We are antipodean, and therefore bluff; irony has little place in our poetic personality. And where older forms are attempted, they are often misused; witness Fitz-Gerald's attempt, in 'Essay on Memory', to wrench the heroic couplet to a task for which it is by nature unfitted. Judith

Wright may appear to use, in 'Bullocky', a similar stanza form
to that which we find in Eliot's 'Sweeney Among the Nightin-
gales'. Yet no two poems could differ more in the uses to which
they put that form. They produce two utterly differing movements, two quite dissimilar emotional climates. And the difference is more than a personal one, existing between two individual
poets; it is a difference between two societies and traditions.

It is in imagery and diction that part of the English example
was followed by Australian poets. There is no need to demonstrate the claim that the past thirty years have seen a gradual
increase in the use of colloquial speech rhythms, even of speech-
idioms, of relaxed and varied lines, and of a more native
imagery. The revised attitude to imagery has been particularly
interesting. In the first place, it has not gone as far in the
direction of sheer allusiveness as Eliot and his disciples have
gone, although it has certainly become wider in scope, firmer
and richer in application. But, above all, it has become localized;
which is to say that it concerns itself with man largely in terms
of his natural landscape, and so is limited by the need to conform to the typical details of that landscape. Judith Wright is
more deeply concerned with nature symbolism than most of our
modern poets; yet her practice does stand for something constant in the atmosphere of their poetry :

> Tunnelling through the night, the trains pass
> in a splendour of power, with a sound like thunder
> shaking the orchards, waking
> the young from a dream, scattering like glass
> the old men's sleep; laying
> a black trail over the still bloom of the orchards.
> The trains go north with guns.
>
> Strange primitive piece of flesh, the heart laid quiet
> hearing their cry pierce through the thin-walled cave
> recalls the forgotten tiger
> and leaps awake in its old panic riot;
> and how shall mind be sober,
> since blood's red thread still binds us fast in history?
> Tiger, you walk through all our past and future,
> troubling the children's sleep; laying
> a reeking trail across our dream of orchards.

Here is an example of what Mr Devaney would presumably call modernism in Australian poetry. Everything about it would seem to proclaim its errant contemporaneity: the urgent colloquial-seeming movement, the lines of varied length, the liberal use of its basic metre, the omission of the capital at the beginning of each line: the contemporary sense of fact, the mention of machinery, the use of strongly 'unpoetic' words such as 'reeking', the determination that the heart shall be shown not as an instrument of feeling nor as a mere figure of speech, but as a physical and barely defended organ. If such things as these constitute the dread disease, then Miss Wright has a bad dose of it. And yet the poem has nothing of the great variety, the ever-present sophistication of Eliot and Auden; its opposing symbols are frank and open – are indeed obvious; its diction is not that of the experimentalist, but of common speech exalted and even a little strained; the imagination is here liberated by its very roots in fact, in the sensuous present. And above all, its tone is un-English, not in the least derived from a climate of cosmopolitan talk, such as we get in Auden, for example:

> In Brueghel's *Icarus,* for instance: how everything turns away
> Quite leisurely from the disaster; the ploughman may
> Have heard the splash, the forsaken cry,
> But for him it was not an important failure; the sun shone
> As it had to on the white legs disappearing into the green
> Water; and the expensive delicate ship that must have seen
> Something amazing, a boy falling out of the sky,
> Had somewhere to get to and sailed calmly on.

I do not know a single Australian poet who could have written this; indeed, I do not think I know a single one who would have wanted to. The two pieces I have quoted are, of course, very individual; and neither of them represents its author at his best. Yet when we place them together, they exemplify much of the difference between the conceptions of poetry in the two countries. It is a difference at once of intellectual adventurousness and of emotional tone. Slessor's considerable variety of rhythm, his virtuosity of image, and his liking for the startling conceit, are unusual in this country. So is his predilection for city life and its characteristic imagery. Since Brennan's droning tram swung westward, and Furnley Maurice's city markets recollected themselves in tranquillity, urban imagery has been permissible in Australian poetry; but it has never become general. Where it has been used to any effect, it has often been used in a spirit either of whimsy or of incipient fantasy. Slessor and those who have followed his example romanticized (or, if I may make a barbarous coinage – aestheticized) it into the figures of a dream landscape. Even with the added, modern hardness of image, even with the rhythms following those of speech, they gave us an impressionistic poetry in which everything but the momentary detail was excitingly blurred. Slessor's John Benbow, gazing rakishly in the Sydney shops, has nothing in common, either in the quality of his nostalgia or in the degree of his sophistication, with the crowds of Eliot's London :

> Unreal City,
> Under the brown fog of a winter dawn,
> A crowd flowed over London Bridge, so many,
> I had not thought death had undone so many.
> Sighs, short and infrequent, were exhaled,
> And each man fixed his eyes before his feet.

For, whatever its new freedom and hardness, Australian imagery is natural imagery. Our modernism (if we are entitled to call it so) has been dominated, not by the demands of literary experiment, but by the constant effort to adjust our imaginations first to the brute fact of Australia, and then to the spiritual fact of man living in Australia. The result was a broadness, an expansiveness, a naïve naturism, growing up at the very moment when England was committing herself either to the virtues of subtle precision and narrowness, or to those of the treatment of landscape in terms derived from the surrealists. So, if our poetry has been lacking in sophistication and formal adventurousness, it has been lacking also in the brittleness which sophistication is apt to produce.

So far I have been writing as though English poetry of the past thirty-five years were a land dominated by Eliot. That impression is an entirely false one; and I could never have encouraged it had not the demands of comparative judgment forced such an encouragement on me. If Eliot was the Caesar to this land, it like Gaul was subsequently divided into three parts;

or at least it was subject to three revolts, if we include Eliot's own. English modernism seems to have generated a vitality of its own – a vitality which has not been without its signs of distraction and neurotic anxiety for change. Its changeability is, indeed, one of its greatest enemies. Auden's revolt, and the revolt of the thirties in general, had two grounds of complaint; first, that Eliot's investigation of the contemporary scene was made in a vacuum, without a proper sense of the social context and of the political significance in the breakdown of civilization; and, second, that it left no room for recommendations to positive action, either social or cultural. Hence the growing insistence on psychological terms, on a more direct presentation of contemporary facts, on a more direct investigation of contemporary themes, on more warmth of feeling. Hence the occasional jazz-rhythms, the direct and explosive irony, the vast increase in the range and ambiguity of images.

But if *they* thought Eliot arid they too were to be accused of aridity in their turn. Auden is no longer the insurgent; he is no longer even head of the army of occupation. For after him came the neo-Romantics, infiltrating in small groups each of which seemed likely to produce at any moment the badge of its own ridiculous high-sounding title. Their complaint was that Auden and his friends were dealing with a partial view of man, and that this was the reason for the aridity in the verse of the thirties.

Now, these people hold most of the field,[3] and it would be as well to glance at them for a moment. They are not a movement, they are a tendency – or, rather, a brace of tendencies, which taken together do not quite add up to a movement. There is a Surrealist wing, and there is a wing which leans on the air of a revived romantic sentiment. And they are as different in their rashness as Auden is different from Eliot. Yet they share certain things, certain traits, certain unformulated principles of poetic action.

In the first place, they have inaugurated a new reign of poetic diction, after the colloquialism of the thirties. It is a diction dif-

[3] Although they are now being challenged by a group of young 'wits' who owe much of their inspiration to William Empson, and who seem likely to offer us a remedy much more dangerous (because more boring) than the disease itself.

ferent in kind from that which Wordsworth characterized as a 'gaudy and inane phraseology'. Instead of personifications, generalized properties, and classical allusions, these poets rest on a use of certain pattern of images as having a symbolic effect; they use words as talismans, in an almost magical or at least animistic way.

In the second place, they have sought, despite notable defections in their ranks,[4] to produce passion by oblique means. They use variants of the objective correlative not to redirect passion, but to simulate or produce it. The consequence is a poetry which on the whole disdains, or uses with contemptuous casualness, *both* thought and strong feeling; it exists as though passion were felt to reside in images, or to be magically attached to them, rather than to be the cause and moulder of them. I speak harshly about this poetry; and perhaps I speak of it in a hasty and sweeping way; yet it is the poetry which dominates the present English periodicals and anthologies, at least in places where the editors are not still bemused by the beauties of reportage; and I feel it to be, despite the claims made for it, a rather inhuman poetry. Neo-Romanticism acts in literature as the blood does in certain physiological states. The sensations, and the images which they generate, tend to devour ideas and feelings in much the same way as, in the disease of leukaemia, the red corpuscles swallow the white.

There has been nothing of this changeability, nothing of its concomitant extravagance, in the work of Australian poets. This may be one of the reasons why it is difficult to feel enthusiastic about any new development in our poetry; but it is nevertheless a good sign rather than a bad. If we are awkward and to a degree dull, it is with the dull awkwardness of the youth who is content to grow under his own powers, at his own rate, and who will not be pushed; it is not that other disguised (because distracted) dullness of the middle-aged neurotic. There have been no revolts, few explosive changes, almost no manifestos. Life is still real in Australia (though perhaps not overly real); and it is very, very earnest.

I do not want to convey the impression that our poetry has been, during the period of its most rapid and significant growth

---

4 Dylan Thomas is a good example.

(the past three decades), completely insulated from overseas influence. Such a contention would be ridiculous. Australian poetry does not possess some magical property, which nobody can exactly name, for developing without air and sun and water from outside. It would be foolish to deny that something did happen to our poetry in the late twenties of this century; something happened to its characteristic shapes and emphases, something began to happen to its diction and sense of symbolism; and whatever happened was connected, partly as a product, with the beginnings of modernism in English poetry a short time before.

Yet the connection was of an indecisive kind, as it concerned both the influence of individual on individual, and the influence of imaginative climate on climate. Slessor was possibly influenced by Eliot, as Judith Wright was later to be more firmly influenced; Joseph O'Dwyer and Bertram Higgins were possibly so close to Eliot that we may see them as disciples, but their poetry has been in any case of little influence; McAuley was affected by Yeats, but he was affected quite as much by Blake, whom no one can accuse of the perversions of modernism. The web of relationships and influences and debts is indecisive and hard to discern. We cannot estimate, in fact, what lasting influences modernism has had on our poetry at all. For most of our poets, whatever influence was exerted came not through the transmission from one country to another of a radical aesthetic doctrine or a basic creative method. It was exerted, rather, through the atmosphere of creative life and critical sternness alike, which the leading English reformers had created about them – an atmosphere in which, for Australian poets as much as for the English, the soft optimism of the Tennysonians and the muscular cheerfulness of the Georgians could no longer be considered a central poetic tradition. It is this atmosphere which no doubt accounts largely for the hardness and sense of adventure which had come into our poetry. Yet its influence was not exerted tyrannically, not even directively, but simply as a guarantee of poetic balance. And within it, being subject to its wind and sun and air, Australian poetry developed according to obscure laws of its own.

The development was slow, and the more startling touches of

modernism on it were greeted and casually accepted. So, while continuing to go his own way, the Australian poet added a few tricks to his repertoire, and became at times rather sloppy and subjective in the recording of his sensations. But whatever harm has been done has been peripheral; nothing of the core has been eaten away. The dangers of Australian poetry still come from insularity rather than from an unrestrained spirit of experiment; and life on a very large island does not of itself tend toward solipsism. In truth, our poetry is still in a very real sense domestic; it has a flavour of cooking about it, or at least a certain smokiness of the kitchen; it is not attuned to tragic realities, or even to the existence of any tragic dimension in experience; it is uncomfortable in the neighbourhood of the soul, and obviously prefers the sensations, so long as they are discreetly accounted for and pleasingly arranged. Judith Wright deals with things of primal significance as much as any of our poets, yet none of her poems has much of the complexity of mind, the experimental probing of the resources of language in order to reinforce meaning, which we find in Hopkins and even in Yeats. There is a largeness of one kind present in Australian work – a largeness of gesture and of image; but there is a largeness of a different kind missing – the largeness of the soul confronting its destiny in a present which has become suddenly tragic. If that largeness, the largeness of magnanimity, is the criterion of great poetry, then ours is puny beside Hopkins and Yeats. Happily, however, there are other criteria, and other qualities which do a certain amount to compensate.

The nature of our development itself is not easy to see, and the tenets behind it (if indeed there were tenets at all) are even more difficult of discernment. I have already said that the ideas which motivated the work of the Australian twenties were sketchy, ill-defined, and apparently immature. It is probably in the thirties that the real technical advances were made. R. D. FitzGerald has summarized the difference between the two decades in a pithy and even aphoristic way. He has said 'In the Twenties, we tried to portray *things* concretely; in the Thirties, we extended our scope, and tried to portray ideas concretely'. This was said in conversation, and is all the better for it; at any rate, I feel sure that he will not object to having his ideas reported, even when the report carries the risk of its own distortion. And the aphorism does express a good deal of the truth of his own poetic development – even, to a lesser extent, of the development of other men. There is little significant change over ten years in the spirit of FitzGerald, or of Slessor, or of Hugh McCrae; but there is a considerable change in their development of the resources of language. Their poetry of the thirties does become harder, more masculine, and in some sense more intellectual, for it is grappling more closely, albeit quite obscurely, with ideas as well as with things. Paradoxically, the later poetry of all these men shows an advance not only in mental substance, but also in the hardness, the directness, with which they portray *things*. Their poetry which had been concerned mainly with things turns out to have been concerned to an alarming extent with sensations and sentiments; it is the expanding mind which has led to the more exact image.

And their example has been followed and extended, notably by Douglas Stewart and Francis Webb. Other poets, such as Brian Vrepont, John Thompson, McAuley, and Judith Wright, stem from different imaginative stocks; yet their use of images fused with their governing ideas extends, and in a sense ratifies, the experiments of their elders. I am not for a moment pretending that our modern poetry is homogeneous, much less monolithic; but it does share throughout its two generations something of a common hardening, a common attempt at realism. It is in the service of this consistent development that our poetry has gained in colloquial emphasis, in richness of texture, and in variation of rhythmic movement.

But that attempt is in a fairly narrow sense technical; there is more than that to the development which our poetry has undergone. We have not been, however secretly and individually, following a mere technical prescription; we have also been engaged in a spiritual enterprise. If our imagery has developed, if our idiom has become more varied and exact, it is because we have been learning spiritual things. We have come to be concerned less with the insensate paraphernalia of our environment than with its human significance, and with the land less as a backdrop or as the stimulant of our sentiments and sensations than as the milieu of, and a force in, our attempts to be more fully human. As I have said elsewhere, Australian poetry over the past fifteen years has become more conscious of its spiritual potentialities, as of its place in a European tradition; it has become more endued with human values; and while it has become less self-conscious, it has gained in conscious realism. John Thompson, for example, has spoken of the bush as 'This wary, gaunt, oracular bush'; such a phrase would have been virtually impossible to a poet of the twenties, just as it would have been inconceivable to Bernard O'Dowd; for it is a phrase in which a judgment, an assessment, is implied, as well as a response; it shows an increase in technical maturity because it bespeaks an increase in objectivity.

Whatever technical developments have taken place, therefore, have taken place as the result of a process, more implicit than open, of thinking out the issues which face Australian man. And it is necessary to add that such developments have not yet come to dominate the poetic scene. They have been met, and to a degree counteracted, by other forces: one is the force of nationalism, the other is the force of cosmopolitanism.

The first of these is the more powerful, if not in the production of poetry, at least in its politics. The *Bulletin, Southerly,* the *Jindyworobak Anthologies,* and the publications of the Left-Wing poets, are all, in their various ways, the strong points of a fervour which can justly be described as nationalist. The reliance on a naïve and partly propagandist rhetoric in some of these publications, the reactionary preference for verse of the great outback or for 'ballad' forms in the others, produce an imaginative climate in which a richly spiritual poetry is difficult, and formal experiment almost impossible. I do not want to deal *seriatim* with these schools or tendencies; I am convinced that, on the whole, they are a retarding influence on the development of our poetry; the *Bulletin* and *Southerly,* of course, publish a certain amount of good poetry; but I am referring not only to their creative, but also to their critical practice. As for the Jindyworobaks and the 'social realists', they often give the impression of wishing to circumscribe poetic forms in an alarmingly complete way. One gets from them a view of the Australian tradition which is absurd in critical emphasis and extremely restrictive in poetic practice. It is as though they were insisting that there are certain moods, certain ideas, certain poetic forms (such as the ballad and the ballad-lyric) which are inherently Australian, and therefore central, definitive, sacrosanct. Such a suggestion is both ridiculous and doctrinaire; it has nothing in common with the real aspirations, joys, and agonies of our people; it smells of a mingling of sweat and the hothouse.

The other tendency has almost disappeared, at least as a present creative force. It is the tendency associated with the names of Max Harris and the publication *Angry Penguins*. One can only regard the humiliation of the first and the demise of the second as both exemplary and untimely. Their poetry recognized no local allegiances, no directly social roots, no necessity for what it is normally possible to call realism. It was the only parallel in Australia to the neo-Romanticism of the English forties. Fortified by the Surrealist experiments, rooted in casual sensation, brimming with a sentiment recognizably romantic and nostalgic, it did nevertheless generate a certain poetic excitement. It seems, on the whole, to have been thinner and more brittle than its lush English counterpart; yet it did have, running uneasily beneath its surface anarchism, a power of what can only be described as moral earnestness.

Such an attempt at an advanced cosmopolitanism may have been brash; it has certainly seemed rash to many people. Yet it is important to realize that Harris at least was no doctrinaire; and while his magazine lasted, it had at least the negative effect of combating, by a stringent and forthright criticism, the rhetorical and formal ineptitude of its enemies the nationalists. Now it is gone, and Harris with it; nationalism holds too much of the field — and struts, where it cannot dance, on that uneasy surface.

Something of a more positive tradition remains too, and it is being at once enriched and extended. I should like, very briefly, to make the attempt of characterizing it, at the conscious risk of seeming to enclose it in a formula. Despite the apparent modernness of the best among our contemporary poets, they seem to me to stand somehow in an older tradition. The central strains of Australian poetry, ever since the nineties of last century, have been the lyrical and the rhetorical — the twin notes of song and declamation which are not unnatural friends

in a young country very conscious of its own national status
and anxious to understand itself, so long as understanding can
be procured with the minimum of imaginative and intellectual
effort.

The coming of federation may be taken as a landmark, though
hardly as a cause. At the turn of our century, we find rhetoric
abounding, in good poetry and in bad, in the high places as in
the low. We find, for example, O'Dowd's quasi-mystical poems
on nationhood cheek by uneasy jowl with the more rigorous
eloquence of his long poem, 'The Bush'. We find Christopher
Brennan, possibly the greatest heart and mind of all Australian
poets, eloquently pursuing his fate through the sorrowful wastes
of the universe. We find William Baylebridge pursuing *his*
through a thicket of notions and conceits. And we find McCrae,
inhabitant of a more physical thicket, shouting of the great god
Pan.

These are the chief voices of our century's first two decades;
and they are all declaiming. Beside them, others are trilling or
piping – Dame Mary Gilmore, and John Shaw Neilson, and
at least the ghost of Victor Daley. Others of lesser note are
attempting to combine the two traditions – rhetoric and song. I
take it the emergence of a kind of ballad-lyric was an attempt at
such a combination.

Such, at least, seems to me to have been the tradition – a
naïve but open-hearted one. All in all, it gave considerable
impetus to a poetry which had just been freed from its depen-
dence on English or on outback models. It also provided a
tradition of high and ringing statement which the so-called
'modernists' were later to follow, often unconsciously. There is
much of the rhetorician about FitzGerald and Slessor, even
about McAuley and Judith Wright. If it is moreover a less conscious, a less public rhetoric, that is all to the good. The twin
strains themselves, of rhetoric and song, have been combined
in much of our modern poetry; and certainly it has not proved
very difficult to assimilate the modern experiments, limited as
they are, to this tradition.

Australian poetry is quite unlike English in this respect: that
it is expansive, extravert, a poetry of decided gestures. Even the
more openly intellectual poetry shows it, at least as a tendency;

and the existence of the tendency itself, of its consistency and importance, will have to be taken into account in the poetry which is to be written tomorrow.

What form that poetry is to take must for the present be obscure. What technical developments it is to embrace, what technical resources our present poetry can lend it, are matters of the merest conjecture. I am not myself a nationalist, in any sense of the word; and, perhaps to an unreasonable extent, I despise nationalism in poetry. I feel very keenly the absence of intellectual power, the absence of a developed sense of spiritual destiny, in the bulk of our poetry. For me, these things are not only critical necessities, they are constant personal preoccupations. I cannot help feeling that we must look towards Asia and towards Europe at once; the gaze which the spiritual meaning of history enjoins on us is that of Janus with his double face. Formally, technically, we must learn from Europe: not directly, by way of imitation, but indirectly, by reason of our coming to realize just where we stand in the European tradition. Technical developments are valuable only if they are first spiritual ones, interior and personal and profound. And such a spiritual awakening must include a new awareness, a properly cultural and literary awareness, of the powers and needs of Asia.

So much may be said and, through its very portentousness, may mean nothing in terms of practical achievement. What is now possible in Australian poetry I simply do not know. I see a good deal of the verse of the young men, the men who are between five and ten years younger than myself; and I know that they place great stress – I would add, a humble stress – on the necessity for technical resources. They have learnt that poetry is not mere self-expression, that it is a personal task, and that it has something quite intimate to do with their responsibility as men towards their fellow-men. I feel that they are probably wrong in their preoccupation with technique. I do not share the desire which they apparently feel to bring other lives, the lives of obscure and average men, directly into their poetry. However, the best of them are humble and devoted; they are aware of a present deficiency in our poetry; and it may be that they will accomplish something of the technical exploration and stiffening which our poetry needs.

Insofar as their researches *are* technical, I feel that they will learn more from contemporary American poetry than from British. American poetry is at once the more earthy and the more intellectually subtle. It gives us the testimony of a national (though hardly a nationalist) poetry finding its own methods of making spiritual values local. In it, more than in any other poetry of the English-speaking world, values have become converted into style in a way which can provide a valuable lesson to a still younger poetry. But so far the influence of American poetry has been so tentative as to be almost indiscernible. The next two decades ought to see its increase; for the next two decades will be our testing-time.

There is, after all, a positive relationship between intellectual and formal adventure, just as there is between intellectual and formal balance. There would seem to be a connection, for example, between the fact that Douglas Stewart's awareness has not developed significantly and the further fact that his poetic technique has not developed much either. If a poet is satisfied with his intellectual formations, he is likely to be smug about his poetic forms; and if he is satisfied with his characteristic forms, he is hardly likely to become creatively preoccupied with the quality of his thought. The two things run together; they are the twins of Parnassus; it is they whose lives are fused together in that fire which several decades have tacitly agreed not to name inspiration. I think the point is important. In the two cases I can think of where form has been perfected in a moving way, there has also been if not an advance in thought at least a crystallization of it. The two cases are those of FitzGerald and A. D. Hope. And while it is idle to expect that our apprentice poets will follow either of them, at least they may learn from the personal example of them both.

Contemporary Left-Wing Poets

ONE OUGHT, I suppose, to call them Social Realists, for it is the more familiar title; but it is also the less genuinely expressive. For it is doubtful whether most of these poets are Realists at all in any poetic sense; and it is almost as doubtful what their verses have to do with the social life of man as it exists in fact rather than in the artificial scheme of Marxist concepts. So that title will not do, and I am reduced to the notion of 'Left-Wing', to a metaphor of political placing rather than to one which indicates the manner of their poetic contact with society.

And, in fact, I have chosen this term in order to be as little tendentious as possible. One cannot call them Communists, for they are not all members of that party; one cannot call them Socialists without giving the unfortunate impression that *their* kind of poetry is what Socialists commit themselves to when seized in the flush of inspiration.

The term 'Left-Wing' denotes at once a definite political alignment, in which (for our present purposes) I am not very much interested, and a view, more or less definite, of the relationship which exists between poetry and the meaning of the lives of the Australian people. It is this relationship, as a body of fairly heterogeneous work postulates and reveals it, that I wish to consider here. I do not want to be thought of as assessing an uncongenial literary movement from a point somewhere to the political Right of that movement; the question of my position in the absurd and artificial semi-circle of Australian politics is here irrelevant; at the same time, I am concerned with the general failure of the literary expression of that humanism which the Left-Wing poets have adopted as a guide in living and a norm in writing.

And it is, after all, a humanism, though partial, even truncated, and ill-considered. It is an attempt to use poetic forms in order to make meaningful and up-to-date statements about the life of Australian man, of the direction in which that life is tending, and of the principles according to which it must be directed if it is to prove ultimately significant.

Contemporary Left-Wing Poets

53

The first noticeable point is that these poets make use of an older tradition of Australian writing in order to establish at once a social dynamic for their own writing and an emotional atmosphere in which it may be favourably received. And they have a certain right on their side. Left-Wingery with us has not been what it was in England: the concern of a decade; it has been on the contrary a recurrent strain, a constant aspiration, in our poetry. Whether this strain has produced much good poetry is another matter, and one which may be allowed for the moment to lie fallow. Certainly it has not been quite so constant, quite so homogeneous, as the contemporary Leftists would like to believe. In fact, they pin a disproportionate importance on the unwarranted assumption that they are extending, purifying, and completing the central tradition of Australian poetry. They edit anthologies, and give them titles taken from Henry Lawson; they quote on their title-pages poets long dead, with the assumption that they all share essentially the same view of life; Eureka and Ned Kelly become the factitious symbols for a modern political versifying; the bush ballads, and their 'folk origins', have lately become the currency of literary traffic between the Leftists and the readers whom they desire to influence. It is all a pleasant form of self-deception, for there is not a great deal in common between the two movements at all.

The older revolutionary tradition in our poetry was a rather different one from the newer. It was an over-simplified one, with two general wings or tendencies. On the one hand, there were such poets as Henry Lawson and Victor Daley; on the other, there were Bernard O'Dowd and Mary Gilmore. The first pair sang the benefits of mateship and of simple, undoctrinaire aims; the all-too-frequent, indeed all-too-obvious anger in this poetry was an uncomplicated anger at the undoubted oppression of the class to which, by birth or occupation, its writers belonged. It was, in short, an early working-class poetry, helping the working class to grow to a corporate self-consciousness, and tending in its forms to the ballad, the chant, or the 'come-all-ye'. And while the anger was robust enough, while its causes were unmistakably real enough, the positive ideals to which it pointed were vague, the artistic hand (in sketching them) fell too readily into vague gesture, unstabilized by any sufficiently full and satisfying images of the redeemed society. It was too much a poetry of direct statement; and while it insisted rather ponderously on the strength of its own emotions, it did nothing to reveal their complexity or to illumine their source.

The second of the two wings was equally simple in content, but more idealistic in tone; it represented an ideal of the more educated, and was full of idealistic overtones, shot through with the slightly inept melodies of a religious fervour which tended towards pantheism. Like the poetry of Lawson and Daley, it was undoctrinaire, it did not embody definite doctrines of man or of society; yet, unlike them, it showed a greater variety of moods and of poetic forms; it was more philosophical, and it *did* make an attempt to foreshadow the redeemed society. The interesting thing is that the attempt was made in terms either of an out-dated mythology or of Nature and her seasonal changes. Man was seen as growing into political maturity by a process as natural as the change from winter into spring; and the two growths, in fact, tended to be emotionally identified.

The new men are very different. They tend to be middle class rather than working class, and they are not unaffected by the petulance and sense of grievance which are the middle-class revolutionary's substitute for proletarian anger. They are less idealistic and single-minded – a fact which, could I verify it, would no doubt prove surprising to a number of people. Their poetry represents an attempt, made in a social context infinitely more complex and worrying than Lawson or O'Dowd ever knew, to reconcile the image of man suffering with the image of man revolutionary.

If I may anticipate my thesis a little, I should say that the best of them (Manifold, and some of John Thompson and Laurence Collinson) *do* succeed in infusing doctrine into a por-trayal of life which remains, even to the uninitiated, a recogniz-ably human one; others, however, such as Victor Williams, Muir Holburn, and Bartlett Adamson, do tend to avoid a poetic and lively representation of ideas in favour of a doctrinal representa-tion of life, which leaves that life less than we know it in fact to be, and which in the event limits and distorts even its revo-lutionary meaning.

We may compare part of a ballad by Lawson with one by

John Manifold. Lawson's ballad 'Second Class Wait Here' is a
good example of one tendency :

> At suburban railway stations – you may see them as you pass –
> There are signboards on the platforms saying 'Wait here second
>   class';
> And to me the whirr and thunder and the cluck of running gear
> Seem to be for ever saying, saying 'Second class wait here –
>   Wait here second class
>   Second class wait here'.
> Seem to be for ever saying, saying 'Second class wait here'.
>
> Yes, the second class were waiting in the days of serf and prince,
> And the second class are waiting – they've been waiting ever
>   since.
> There are gardens in the background, and the line is bare and
>   drear,
> Yet they wait beneath a signboard, sneering 'Second class wait
>   here'.
>
> I have waited oft in winter, in the mornings dark and damp,
> When the asphalt platform glistened underneath the lonely
>   lamp,
> Glistened on the brick-faced cutting 'Sellum's Soap' and
>   'Blower's Beer',
> Glistened on enamelled signboards with their 'Second class wait
>   here'.
>
> And the others seemed like burglars, slouched and muffled to
>   the throats,
> Standing round apart and silent in their shoddy overcoats;
> And the wind among the poplars, and the wires that thread
>   the air,
> Seemed to be for ever snarling, snarling 'Second class wait here'.

There is no need to continue the quotation; the ballad, as it
proceeds, comes to vary neither in tone nor in tempo. We may
pass to Manifold's 'The Last Scab of Hawarth':

> Why does the fire burn high to me
> When your end burns so low?
> Maybe it's of the coal I cut
> Fifteen years ago.
>
> What are the sparks that fly so far
> And flash against the dark?
> They might be eyes that would not see
> When we went out to work.

There's five men went scabbing then
And thought their work was well,
And one died mad and two died sane,
And one that's dead in jail.

There's five men went scabbing then
And thought their work was fit,
And sane or mad there's four men dead
And one that's living yet.

And maybe if they haddna worked
When all the rest stood by,
The coal that's aye so cheap to work
Might not be so dear to buy.

And maybe if they haddna worked
When all the rest stood back,
The fire might keep and the kids might sleep
And the night be not so black.

There's two died sane and two died mad
And the one that's last is me.
And he went with a clothes-line in his hand
To look for a leaning tree.

Both of these are simple in theme and development, both of them are in some sense simple message-poems. But there the similarity ends. Lawson is completely absorbed in his message as in a personal experience, and so does not try to organize it for greater effectiveness. Manifold on the other hand is a conscious literary artist, and has a fair deal of the artist's suavity and premeditation. His poem seems to me a very good political ballad, even though it does not exhort anybody to do anything at all, and is completely devoid of agonized clichés like 'iron throats' and 'rivers of fists'. It has most of the devices of the traditional balladist – easy alliteration, occasional half-rhymes, an internal rhyme in the third line to tighten some stanzas, a slight recasting in two or three successive stanzas of the central point he is making; and yet it has, too, minor shifts in pace and tone, a number of minor subtleties of rhythm, which enable him to display his message in the most strategically apt way. It is a poem concerned with a strategy at once political and poetic, a carefully didactic art. We may notice, for example, the way in which the first stanza sets the scene, and at the very same time tells us something of the poem's message as it is later to appear:

> Why does the fire burn high to me
> When your end burns so low?
> Maybe it's of the coal I cut
> Fifteen years ago.

Such a ballad bears the same relation to Lawson's as an art-song based on a folk tune bears to the folk-song itself. It is an essentially literary ballad, and fairly entreats us to deal with it in literary terms. I need not say that this fact strengthens, rather than weakens, its didactic, political purpose.

But those are ballads – and the ballad is no longer a very persuasive poetic form. It is necessary to look at certain other tendencies in our contemporary Left-Wing poetry.

Here we must continue to bear in mind that my present interest in them is largely an interest in a group of men who are communally committed to a view of life and society, and to a view which claims to be a positive, dynamic one in terms of human aspirations; in other words, a specific kind of humanism. Now, if we look at them under this aspect, we shall be particularly interested in seeing whether they manage to bring together, in the one poetic formulation, we might even say the one unified poetic universe, both man's objective and his subjective worlds. I think that, on the whole, they fail markedly to do so; in fact, Manifold seems to me to be the only one of the whole group who makes any considerable attempt to do so. For reasons which I shall outline later and which poetically are not entirely creditable, I find his attempt successful.

One of the most curious and significant things about all these men, except Manifold, is the fact that they make a distinct cleavage between the inward and outward worlds of man; the poetry in which they attempt to express the former seems to have little in common, either in general style or in emotional attitude, with the poetry in which they express the latter. The very texture of the poetry as a whole reveals a divided intention and interest, in each man an almost schizoid sensibility. The poetry of social protest and analysis derives little of its emotional heightening or individuality from any profound awareness of their own inward states; the 'private poetry' on the other hand tends to a kind of slack Wordsworthianism. Collinson, Holburn, Williams and Thompson seem to have two almost totally separate poetic worlds, and in neither of them is their sensibility fully engaged. Two poems by Laurence Collinson may be compared to sharpen the point; it should appear all the sharper in virtue of the fact that, of the four poets I have mentioned, he is the one who seems least radically affected by this division of attention.

Here, first of all, is a poem to Ethel and Julius Rosenberg, killed, 19 June 1953:

> Dead. Not all our million puny souls
> sufficed to make the truthful giant live
> and rise, enraged, and smite and smite the false
> despised beasts. Not all that we could give,
> not all our hearts could move him into life
> to stride into those cruel outrageous lands
> where innocence was murdered. Man and wife;
> they waited to be saved. And now confess;
> We did not do enough; we loved but failed;
> they loved us more than life, yet we loved less,
> and snarling hypocritic death prevailed.
> But grief in growing gives our power increase;
> they shall return in our every act of peace.

It is a poor, uncertain, distracted poem, even on the level of propaganda – largely, I suppose, because it poses the issue in false terms, or, rather, poses as a moral issue what is not really one at all. I could have quoted better political poetry by Collinson, but it would have been 'political' in a substantially different sense. If this poet is saved from a complete dissociation of sensibility, it is because he has a deep ironic quality which does not allow him too consistently to see things in colours of glaring opposition. Another sonnet by him reveals, however, a completely different world:

> Because I love, I misinterpret these:
> the normal gesture and the friendly glance.
> With every softened syllable I seize
> a prologue to an amorous advance.
> Because I love, your every word is truth;
> unreason fled when first it heard you speak;
> beside yours, others' virtues are uncouth –
> perfection does not seem so far to seek.

Because I love, I sigh away the sun;
maybe write a poem, sometimes cry,
and argue, and make jokes with you, but shun
all words to prove I care that you are by.
O in the night, when logic is the heart,
you take me in your arms and play your part.

Here, as I have said, are two separate worlds of feeling, even of imagination. The first is a harsh, generalized world, with an over-insistent force, as though the poet is insisting overmuch on his own political masculinity, his own orthodoxy. The other is one revealed by subtle rhythms, a gentle tone, a sense of truth, of validity, in the investigation of a typical human emotion. It is by no means poetry of the first rank; but it *is* a poetry which bends and becomes flexible under the poet's necessity to be truthful to his own experience, which he recognizes as typical and important; and it is, in consequence, more genuinely passionate than its companion poem. The same is true of Thompson, as we shall see later, and it is true even of such a random versifier as Victor Williams, whose energies would seem at first sight to have been completely canalized into a functional propaganda poetry.

There seems to be no one style, not even one constant view of experience, which can adequately encompass both dominant themes, both recurrent movements of the soul. It seems that protest, social affirmation, righteous indignation, must be shown as such, must be conveyed to the reader unalloyed, unweakened by any other emotion. As for private poetry, poetry of mood and personal feeling, it is as though the poet, exhausted by the task of keeping a stiff upper lip and gritted teeth in the face of the social struggle, sat down to unburden himself, and was all the more passive and be-slippered in consequence.

The truth is that, in so far as these poets recognize the duty of being not only poets, but Left-Wing poets, they write a public poetry, a poetry of public address. I do not mean by this that they necessarily write rhetoric, in its derogatory modern sense; but I do mean that they write a poetry designed to evoke certain appropriate responses in a specific audience, and to be (to the world at large) a witness to some general truth. I am not doubting their sincerity, but I *am* doubting the efficacy, even the general application, of this kind of verse. Collinson and Thompson must know that imagery and tone, which cannot help appearing forced and exaggerated to the uninitiated critic (like myself) will appear to the politically initiated as an apt and readily translatable shorthand. Take, for example, two passages from John Thompson's poem 'The Traveller'. Here is a passage from Section III:

> But it is active joy,
> pushing through scrub, to feel the bush no ghost –
> an angular presence, elbowy, lean as famine,
> dry-rasping, hot with prickles; topping a crag,
> to greet the satin sea where one white sail
> glides like a fin; rolling in sand as fine
> as table salt, or inland on a desert
> standing at midnight opposite the moon
> to find afresh that the elements are four
> not ninety-two. I count them by their feel,
> think with my nose and skin, alive not dying.

Leaving aside the echoes from Auden and the rather involved syntax of that section, we may find in it a savour, may feel the pressure of a definite sensibility at every point in it. Now, here is Section VI of the same poem:

> Alive at every nerve-end I was yet
> sundered from workers, islanded from struggle;
> but, in this wary gaunt oracular bush,
> in tawdry towns and among shacks and humpies
> of an Australia often wrecked or neglected,
> I know my proper comrades – farmer, scientist,
> miner, mechanic, timbergetter, seaman,
> intelligent woman, artist, and ardent child.
> These will construct a dynamic synthesis –
> not by obedience, tolerance, and unfaith,
> but by workmanlike actions of liberation
> worthy of them who first set axe to gum-butt,
> who shimmer-crazy died in drinkless deserts,
> or reached the inland grass with flocks and herds.
> I march, for better or for worse, with them.[1]

[1] This is quoted from *Sesame*, and is preferred to a later and tidier version in *Thirty Poems*, since it shows the poet actually working under political influence.

The movement of this section has something in common with
that of the earlier one, but the diction has changed utterly. However, no terrible beauty has been born. The earlier one was part
of the emotional context of the whole poem; this one seems something removed from that context, something existing on its own
in an emotional void. And yet the clumsy abstractions ('islanded
from struggle', 'construct a dramatic synthesis', and so on) *are*
a recognizable shorthand, and no doubt seem poetically effective
to those who can translate them into mental poetry of their own.
My complaint is that the poet ought not to require them to do
such a work of translation; for the translation involves not only
an intellectual assent to what Thompson is saying, not only an
emotional assent either, but a close familiarity with this shorthand and an assent to the proposition that it is the most appropriate, and hence the most moving shorthand for the expression
of such ideas. Consequently it appeals not as poetry, but as something else – I might add, something less. Thompson himself
speaks of 'workmanlike actions of liberation'; and it ought not
to sound like a piece of unnecessary sarcasm if I say that the
'workmanlike actions' needed for the 'liberation' of poetry are of
a different order from those he has here engaged in. They are
more like the writing displayed in the earlier passage which I
quoted, and which, in its movement, tone, and phrasing, shows
the freshness of a genuine individuality, an unforced excitement.

In one of his satirical poems, John Manifold speaks of the
function of the revolutionary poet in the following terms:

> Verse is the chain of words in which to bind
> The things we wish most often brought to mind.
> Think of an ore new-fossicked, sparse and crude;
> Stamped out and minted, it will buy your food,
> Cajole a mistress, soften the police,
> Raise a revolt, or win ignoble peace,
> Corrupt or strengthen, sunder or rejoin;
> Words are the quartz, but poetry's the coin.

For, as he explains elsewhere in the same poem,

> No man exists but song can touch his mind
> And make him proudly conscious of his kind.

It is a prescription which he does not always follow himself,
and to which in any case I shall be returning. But the point is

obvious. Poetry for Manifold should tend toward song, toward
the exultant lilt, and its effect should be to strengthen a general humanist awareness. Consequently, there *need* be no
cleavage between public and private poetry. For Thompson
and most of the others, however, the conception is clearly
different. Poetry is to be either the expression of personal
mood, in most cases unrelated to any social context or belief,
or a declaration and a gesture of solidarity in an exclusively
socio-political struggle. So it tends either to the warmly wistful
or to the bony and rugged. And both types of verse put together
exclude too much of human experience. Victor Williams and
one or two others, who carry this tendency to its unfortunate
extreme, seem actually to be locked in a tiny cell of facts and
emotions every bit as redolent of the hot-house as the ivory
tower which they scorn:

> Storm rides out of the North-East,
> To plunge at Glen Davis pit.
> And Wall Street speaks through Menzies,
> 'That is the end of it!'
> 'Our country's strength', say the miners.
> 'This oil can keep us free;
> The blood-soaked boots of the oil-kings
> Would trample our liberty.
> And they would ring our country
> With an atom-blasted sea.
> Hold fast with us', say the miners
> 'To our nation's destiny.'
>
> Storm warning! Storm warning!
> Call the Glen Davis men.
> Storm warning! Storm warning!
> Yes, we will answer them.

I am not drawing attention to the poverty of the technique,
but to the factor which goes some distance toward explaining
that poverty. Williams is speaking from a cramped world of
fantasy, and is dealing in the tarnished currency of that world.
He is constructing political myths for the Australian workers;
but in doing so he is presenting not what is the case, but what
he would like to be the case. Indeed, he is pretending that what
ought to be is identical with what is. This is the very opposite of
realism; and it is the danger of a great deal of this poetry,

because it is not the product of the whole man. It is interesting, too, that their expressions of such feelings as anger, impotence, disgust and fear are more real, more imaginatively realized than their rather strained exultation. Marxists, who claim to be the only true philosophical realists, appear to have no conception of the fruitful association of mind and senses which poetry is able to reveal. The minds of Marx and Lenin seem to have been distressingly literal (though not necessarily realistic) ones. And they seem to have affected their poetic followers in an alarmingly forceful way. If there were any drama left in the events at Glen Davis after Victor Williams had been to work on them with his artificial conceptualizing, the humourless and non-dramatic image of Wall Street speaking through the Australian Prime Minister would batter even that remnant into limp acquiescence.

Very little of this is true of John Manifold, because his whole poetic personality seems to move naturally in the world to which he is by philosophy committed. There is very little of the inward life at all. Of all these poets, he is most completely committed in imagination to a world in which things, persons, and ideas are hard and sharply outlined:

> Because this paint is not the shadow of branches
> But dies like a fish on the concrete in the sun's glare,
> Leaving the mechanical outline bare
> To fool only the plane's mechanical glances;
>
> Because this bonhomie is a skinny false
> Mask on the iron skeleton of restraint
> And freedom in newsprint only a smear of paint
> Across the ancient menace, 'Believe, or else . . .'
>
> Therefore if I must choose I prefer to sing
> The tommy gun, the clean, functional thing,
> The singlehander, deadly to the rigid line,
> Good at a job it doesn't attempt to conceal.
>
> Give me time only to teach this hate of mine
> The patience and integrity of the steel.

It is MacNeice made activist. The hate is stated, and its cause adequately implied, but both are fitted into a pattern in which they become properly, that is poetically, identified with the images of steel, paint, and action — images of a man-made world superseding and even challenging, by mocking it, the world of nature. Perhaps this world of his looks a little too much like a gymnasium, but one supposes that gymnasia have their place, for the use even of poets. And it is certain that Manifold does quite well at fitting personal feelings and relationships into this stripped, masculine world. So in another sonnet, this time addressed to Comrade Katharine, he does not cry out or sing, but says brusquely:

> Hands from writing, lips from speech
> Turn to festival with yours,
> Mingle, play, and sleep, and then
>
> Like the sailor to the beach
> Fresh with our united force
> Rally to our task again.

This is a poetry at once sophisticated and vigorous. It is, above all, the poetry of an educated man of adventure, a poetry in which the very texture, the play of word, image, rhythm, and idea, testify to a spirit imaginatively committing itself in action. Perhaps in consequence, the range of possible situations and emotions is narrow – certainly too narrow for poetic fineness or grandeur, though not for occasional good poetry. The constant mood of Manifold's poetic personality (and I take him here as representative of Left-Wing poetry as in all countries it strives to be) is of such a kind that the reverie, the protracted analysis of mental states, can have no place at all. There is simply no room for emotion recollected in tranquillity, for the emotion is always born of the present situation, of a present being met and answered. There is a constant return in his syntax to the present tense, and to verbs of action. At its worst in Manifold, and in other poets, this leads to a kind of tendentious reportage; at its best it leads to the drama of a single action, which may or may not have, either for the poet or for the reader, a symbolic significance. Take, for example, that good taut poem, incidentally and ironically reminiscent of Roy Campbell, 'Fencing-School':

> White to the neck he glides and plunges
> But black above, no human foe
> Pity for whom could rob my lunges
> Of their direction. Faceless, so,

He is no fellow but a show
Of motion purposed to withstand
The blade that sets my nerves aglow
And sings exultant in the hand.

Thus each withdrawn and wide alert,
Focussed on self from hilt to heel,
Nothing breaks in to controvert

The single aim. I only feel
The sinews of my wrist assert
The tremor of engaging steel.

It is the present action, the temporary occupation of mind, will, and senses together, which stirs Manifold to exultation; and the poetry itself shows this, shows it without a quiver of hesitation. Stripped of all but the most necessary adjectives, pinpointed with hard precise verbs, it is a lithe poetry. In all this, as in the work of the other Left-Wing poets, the brotherhood of man and the realities of the social struggle do not become real in terms of the poetry itself, remain either pious intentions behind the poetry or matters for isolated declaration. Manifold cannot show them properly, because they are merely elements in his mind combining with several other elements, and combining with them on equal terms.

There is undoubtedly some significance in the fact that Manifold comes of a wealthy family, and has had athletic training of a sort rather unusual among Australians. Like Thompson, he has spent some years in England, and was a Captain in the British Army. Is it fanciful to see in his work a boyishness, a perennial note of public-school heroism as well as the love of physical engagement as such? These traits would certainly seem to appear in, even to dominate, what is perhaps his best poem, 'The Tomb of Lt. John Learmonth, A.I.F.' The poem begins:

This is not sorrow, this is work: I build
A cairn of words over a silent man,
My friend John Learmonth whom the Germans killed.

There was no word of hero in his plan;
Verse should have been his love and peace his trade,
But history turned him to a partisan.

> Far from the battle as his bones are laid
> Crete will remember him. Remember well,
> Mountains of Crete, the Second Field Brigade!

And it ends:

> I could as hardly make a moral fit
> Around it as around a lightning flash.
> There is no moral, that's the point of it,
>
> No moral. But I'm glad of this panache
> That sparkles, as from flint, from us and steel,
> True to no crown nor presidential sash
>
> Nor flag nor fame. Let others mourn and feel
> He died for nothing: nothings have their place.
> While thus the kind and civilized conceal
>
> This spring of unsuspected inward grace
> And look on death as equals, I am filled
> With queer affection for the human race.

So, in the case of Manifold, there is no problem of a split between the outer and inner lives of man; for him, at least as a poet, the inner life seems hardly to exist—or, if it exists, it does so merely as a reflection on action, a relaxing of nerves, an ephemeral result or occasion of the romantic revolutionary's self-commitment in action. The schoolboy grimly carrying his bat has no leisure for the finer emotions; nor has the revolutionary poet grimly carrying that weapon in the class-war—his art. And although Manifold is seldom grim, although the word 'panache' is as apt of him as it is of his friend, one can never quite miss in his poetry the sense of a man doing things which leave him no leisure for himself.

John Thompson, whom I mentioned earlier, is probably as good a poet as Manifold, and certainly in many respects a more likeable one. But such a judgment rests on his three books of poetry together; and two of these (the first and the third) are patently not the work of a Left-Wing poet at all. It is in his second book, *Sesame*, that country delights begin to be companioned by revolutionary transports; and here he unmistakably offers himself to us as a political poet. Whether we are entitled to speak of his Left-Wingery as contemporary is very doubtful;

but *Sesame* was published not so many years ago. I speak, therefore, only of that book, and of the practical contradictions which
it displays both in purpose and method: a confusion of temperaments so pronounced that one is justified in hazarding the guess
that Thompson, as a poet, was never deeply committed to the
Left-Wing cause at all.

And even in that book, he has his moments, and exercises
his native force. But with him the exercise of that force exhibits
a more strained violence; he seems to find it harder to achieve
the impression of hard, directed action. His is a softer, possibly
gentler sensibility; and consequently his poems often lack a consistent movement and a consistent texture. Verbs are displaced
from the body of the poem in which they appear, and seem over-
insistent. As in this short passage, his impulse is more lyrical,
whereas Manifold is continually and without effort allowing his
sense of endeavour, even extended conceits, to override and
conceal his lyrical surge:

> Out from the little city that chaffers and sweats:
> out from the little villas: out from their fear
> of a naked word or act: out from a soil
> vended or bought by footage: out from Perth:
> out from the suburbs and the mice they breed
> the decorous porch, palm, lawn, and pencil pine
> till vacant lots appear, and ragged yards,
> untidier gardens at the end of paddocks,
> hot scrags of dogged scrub, then rusty workshops,
> the last hotel, the last urban alignment.
> Out, out and up, by orchard slope and vineyard
> (where mouse might lift a forepaw, find a hand)
> till forest hit our nostrils. Behind us now
> the patterned coastlands merge their coloured sweeps
> in argent sunlight, the city dissolves in light
> far off . . .

We must notice the temporarily dominant idea of this poet,
whose words are colloquial, factual, redolent of urban realities;
it is, paradoxically, the idea that city life is insignificant and
cramping compared with the great open spaces. I am sure that
this is not an idea shared by Manifold, or expected of social
realist poets in general. We must notice, too, the rather blurred,
unnecessary violence of parts of the diction ('till forest hit our
nostrils'), a violence and a blurring which *do* seem to be a

recurrent note in the approach these poets make to their experience.

For, all in all, their 'social realist' poetry (to give it finally the title which ought really, I think, to be withheld), that part of their poetry which is distinct from the softer poetry of their private moods and emotions, is a poetry which lives in a hard and rather ungraceful world. There is a hardness and concreteness to their images; and their imagery does, indeed, seem to be more important to them than rhythm or consistency of texture or the careful pitch of the composing voice; it often gives the impression of being gritted out between clenched teeth. One of them speaks somewhere of his poetry being a 'two-fisted defiance' of something or other. It is difficult to imagine poetry being anything of the sort, except indirectly; but the phrase itself is a revealing one. It reveals a determination, a kind of stiff upper-lip concentration on what are considered the essentials of experience, a schoolboy determination very far from what we usually think of as the attitude of the poet to the long apprenticeship which is his life. Too much of it is a poetry of duty. Some of these Left-Wing poets have, in fact, tried to reverse Yeats' dictum : 'We make of the quarrel with others, rhetoric; and of the quarrel with ourselves, poetry'. They do not quarrel sufficiently with themselves; they try to live in a world of the imagination where all is man-made, definite, of hard outlines and definite surfaces, a world for man to grapple with and to wrest to his will. This world excludes a lot; it excludes too much — family, religion, the intactness of nature, certain kinds of direct sensuous and imaginative perception. And to the extent that they succeed in living in it, their poetry is limited, both in profundity and scope, in its own intactness and in its appeal to a circle of readers.

But, of course, they do not completely confine themselves to such a world at all; it is not in the nature of poets to write simply to formulae, even when they are formulae vaguely defined and loosely held. This whole essay in fact has been an attempt to show how they attempt to stick to a formula, and in what way they fail; but they fail, on the whole, not by infusing wider values into the values which they are so determined to hold and to reveal, but rather by separating their poetic sensibilities into two equal halves, like the halves of an orange. Manifold is the exception; he is, I think, a genuine revolutionary poet. Even so, the thing in him which enables him to be so is the very thing which limits and shrinks his poetry; it is a matter, I suppose, of the whole cast of his personality. And even with Manifold, and certainly with the others, the revolution itself is very imperfectly revealed. The brotherhood of man seems in their work little more than an instinct among other instincts, the redeemed society a personal dream or a political programme rather than a poetic presence and reality, even the revolutionary analysis generalized and almost blurred.

Yet it is one modern approach to humanism; it has tempted poetry from three or four mouths; and despite all the mechanical Marxist clamour which accompanies its working, it is not such a frightening dialectic after all. Its bite may be savage, but we have not felt that yet; and its bark is merely a sleepy growl, delivered as it were absent-mindedly between two yawns. Therefore, when it produces a good poet we should consider that a likeable thing indeed; doubly likeable, since we could not have anticipated such an event with any confidence.

A New Bulletin School?

FROM CLOSE observation of the poetry being produced in Australia over the past four or five years, I have come to the uneasy conclusion that a new orthodoxy has been accepted by certain of our editors and poets. The recent appearance of *Australia Writes* and *Australian Poetry, 1953*,[1] brought home, quite dismayingly, not only the extent to which this levelling process has gone, but also the centre of its influence. There can be no doubt that the new 'school', if school it be, is closely connected with Sydney's Labour-baiting *Bulletin;* and that a surprisingly large number of our better-known versifiers are adherents of its precepts.

Statistics, no doubt, prove almost nothing when literature is in question; yet it is surely of some significance that, of the poems reprinted in *Australia Writes,* fifty or more were first published in the *Bulletin,* while the two leading literary journals – *Meanjin* and *Southerly* – are able to chalk up the melancholy totals of three a-piece.

This fact in itself gives little indication of the existence of a '*Bulletin* school' which is coming to dominate Australian poetry; yet when we reflect that there is a well-known *Bulletin* stereotype for verse, and that this is amply reproduced in *Australia Writes,* the statistical fact comes to have a decided cultural importance. No one, I suppose, would accuse T. Inglis Moore of being a *Bulletin* man, but David Campbell is one of the most frequent occupants of the Red Page; and it is David Campbell who apparently had most to do with the choice of poems for *Australia Writes.*

The same pattern of stereotypes is seen, perhaps even more clearly, in *Australian Poetry, 1953.* Within the pages of this annual anthology there seems little that is *not* attributable to the impetus which produces the usual run of Red Page verse.

The general direction of this verse is a return, in far more sophisticated and far more pessimistic terms, to the outback poetry of forty years ago. It is nature poetry; but it is nature

---

[1] *Australian Poetry, 1954,* was no less than staggering in its conformism and lack of taste.

poetry of a particular sort, in which a fondness for and a detailed
observation of natural processes play only a minor role.

> You planted wheat and you reaped white gibbers;
> You ran some sheep but the crows were robbers
> Of eyes and entrails and even the wool
> Plucked from the carcase before it waʳ cool.

Nancy Cato is one of the least capable and convincing among
these writers; and her 'Mallee Farmer' is far from being a good
poem. Yet its very style and quality go a certain distance towards
proving my point. It reads like a summary and a rollicking
parody of one of the main tendencies in the school.

For the important thing about this verse is not so much that it
insists on and incorporates a common style, common images,
but that it reflects a common attitude to life. I am not speaking
of beliefs, for to the large group of poets with whom I am dealing, beliefs seem, unfortunately, an irrelevant luxury. I am
speaking rather of the terms in which they see the spiritual and
social fact of Australia; and it is here that their poetry must be
found inadequate as a creative reflection of Australian life and
aspirations.

This attitude has two main representations. The first I have
already indicated by the simple business of quoting part of a
poem. There is, it is true, a sense of immensity, of tragic possibilities in the very structure of the land itself; yet the tragic
content of these possibilities, though it is often referred to, is
hardly ever recreated and accounted for. Our new outback poets
seem to have taken to heart the words of A. D. Hope – himself,
one would think, a determined enemy of the spiritual tendencies
which they represent:

> They call her a young country, but they lie:
> She is the last of lands, the emptiest,
> A woman beyond her change of life, a breast
> Still tender but within the womb is dry.

But while they have taken these words to heart, they do not
seem interested in making any coherent or hopeful sense of
them; the words have not yet mounted to the poetic head –
which should be their proper repository. So the land is seen as
a desert of heat and glare, the *fons et origo* of vast national

mirages, a place where one can expect to find nothing more rewarding than a few heaps of bones, and an equal number of hawks watching the universe with baleful eyes:

> As I was going through Windy Gap
> A hawk and a cloud hung over the map.
>
> The land lay bare and the wind blew loud
> And the hawk cried out from the heart of the cloud.
>
> Before I fold my wings in sleep
> I'll pick the bones of your travelling sheep,
>
> For the leaves blow back and the wintry sun
> Shows the tree's white skeleton.

This, it is true, is a hymn of praise; for David Campbell, in having a sense of creation, is unlike most of his fellows. Even so, the emphases and the dominant images are typical. In this kind of verse, the hawk population of Australia is clearly and irritatingly larger than the human. Persons, in fact, seem hardly to matter at all, except as objects in a whimsical drama whose action is doomed from the start.

There is obviously something of condescension in this attitude to the general predicament of man, and to his relationship with his physical environment. One would not be unduly begging the question if one located the roots of this condescension in a vague uneasiness, on the part of the poets themselves, about *their own* place in this predicament, their own capacity to do anything at all towards making it intelligible. Incapable of interpreting it, even by an indirect, symbolic method, they tend to ignore it; and they do this by merging man into his physical environment, by giving him a status very little above that of the insect or the mineral kingdom. From the standpoint of the *Bulletin* outback, human beings are in exactly the same order of reality – and, be it stressed, the same order of doom – as the gibber-plains, the mulga, soil erosion, crows, dead sheep, and withered mountains.

This charge is, of course, far too general to be sustained in every case, and I raise it in this manner not in the hope of more easily getting a group conviction and sentence, but to point out the alarming social nature of a symptom which indicates in some members of the school a scarcely-defined tendency, in others a clear and accomplished fact.

In any case, this is only one of the expressions of their flight from the poetic reality of Australia. The other is a more likeable, though by no means a more constructive one. It is seen at its most engaging in the best work of Douglas Stewart himself, and in the more recent poetry of Judith Wright, who seems to be an unwilling mother confessor to the whole school.

> The slim green stem, the head
> Bent in its green reverie;
> So like the first discovery
> Of what the hands could make
> Or spirit dream out of rock
> In the deep gully's shade . . .
>
> All that has come to pass
> Where gum-trees tower in millions
> Lies in the globe of silence
> The little wild orchids hold,
> Lifting each hollow hood
> Nine in a row from the moss.

In itself, this has a decided charm and subtlety of movement. As the expression of one man's vision of reality, it has a place in the evolution of a national culture; but as the assumed mannerism, the chosen attitude of a group, it is significant of a lack of vitality in our poetry. This is the *multum in parvo* view of symbolism to which Judith Wright has recently committed herself. Indeed, it might even be called *omnia in parvulo,* for there is a determined attempt to place the whole of significant reality into the smallest compass possible—and that a compass of inanimate objects. We may be prepared to accept Judith Wright and Stewart in their latest stage of development, and to accept them with a real poetic pleasure; but we would dispense with Brian Vrepont's lizards on rocks, with the well-sinking of Hart-Smith, with the random notations which sometimes seduce David Campbell, with the inept stridencies of Nancy Keesing and Ray Mathew. These two last write as often of the city as they do of the outback; but the general effect is unfortunately the same. We cannot really be consoled or diverted by the unedifying picture of our spiritual ancestors presented by Miss Keesing:

Oh, one from his drowned eyes saw Henry Parkes in a little boat
Go sailing past, and the old man said: 'It's my beard keeps me
    afloat;
When it blows a gale
I use it for a sail.'

Caroline Chisholm swirled in an eddy but her skirts rose bravely
    round:
'Were it not for the air in these hoops,' she said,
'I'd surely be drowned.
I'm far from dead
Though the stone shows '77', she said.

The attempt to shift the outback vision from the heat-glare of
the mulga plains and the cool prettiness of rock-pools results, as
here, in a monstrous clerihew. For Ray Mathew, too, as for Hart-
Smith in some of his moods, Sydney is 'jittery', a dream landscape in which the only real vitality is provided by the background traffic. How far we have come from the vision of
Kenneth Slessor!

These various mutations of the adolescent phoenix reveal, as
I have insisted, a common attitude to Australia and to the task
of recreating in poetry the Australian scene. It is an attitude
of basic incomprehension, escape, sensation-seeking, unacknow-
ledged sadness; and it carries with it a common attitude to poetic
form.

Where the subject is the great outback, we tend to get short
poems, based on certain images which have long since become
clichés, and rocked ineptly in the cradle of a pseudo-ballad metre.
The 'city' poems have a form and movement as slack and
'jittery' as the outlook which they embody. Hart-Smith's poems
of discovery simply repeat, in a devitalized form, the rhythms
and perspectives of Slessor, FitzGerald, and Webb. Only in the
quieter poems about natural objects and scenes glimpsed in
pleasant miniature is there any real variety of form; and this
variety is not a wide one.

But the *tone* of the poetry is quite as significant as its form;
and it is here that the indictment can really be pressed home.
Despite its occasional stridency, its pretence of spiritual urgency,
almost all of this stuff is completely passionless. Not only does
it assign an inferior role to the intellect in the act of creation,
it is actually unable to muster any deep and relevant feeling. Its

predominant tone is one of whimsy, imposed on a structure of
journalistic notations and all-too-easy moralizing:

> And the tiny and almost forgotten violet,
> that knows more of heaven than us all
> put together, receives hot summer without a murmur;
> salutes the frost for what it is;
> bows to the storm, to the violent weather,
> and makes life – now – without recall.
>
> Only a man takes things with the grumble
> yesterday was better; I don't believe
> death was, sex was, drought was, to-morrow was:
> in the beginning in the garden in the good old days,
> everything was lovely without worry without care,
> is all changed. And it's your fault, Eve.

The whimsy here is used in the service of an alleged moral
judgment on life; it also serves to mask the fact that the terms
in which the moral judgment is made are virtually meaningless;
above all, it distracts our attention from the pathetic nature of
the attempt to give the whole business a theological dimension
by importing original sin. It is moralizing, rather than the conversion of deep moral conviction into poetry. It is whimsy rather
than an expression of emotional engagement. It is journalism
of the columnist's type. One would not be surprised to learn that
it had received the collaboration – as it would certainly merit the
endorsement – of such a *jejune* commentator as Mr Eric Baume.

It should not be necessary to insist that whimsy of any sort is
not a suitable staple emotion for a country's poetry; for whimsy
is the great defence of the sentimentalist who is unsure of himself, just as irony is too often that of the sentimentalist who is
cocksure.

There is, then, a school of *Bulletin* poets in a sense that would
not justify us in speaking of a *Meanjin* or a *Southerly* school.
How closely the members of it are connected to one another
by personal ties is irrelevant. There *is* a certain unity, and it
extends both to attitude and to technique; on the whole, it is
a debilitating force in Australian culture – all the more debilitating in that it seems able to command whatever attention it
wishes in our journals and anthologies.

It may be answered that most of the writers I have mentioned, and some others I have not, are unimportant by any standards; and this, of course, is quite true. Judith Wright and Douglas Stewart are good poets; at her best, Miss Wright is very good indeed; but their assumption of the *'Bulletin* manner' has led to their writing too often and in too close a conformity with a formula which itself is easy to manipulate and is ultimately destructive in its effects on the poetic personality. David Campbell, too, seems a genuine poet, as does Roland E. Robinson. Both have a fine, though slight, lyric talent; and they, of all people, can least afford to fall in with a formula of the kind which I have described.

It would be possible to grant to most of the others a certificate of competence; but it would also be irrelevant. The competent manipulation of a formula is not a properly poetic competence at all, even when there are two or three formulae available for alternate use.

The situation itself needs exposing, however, if only because of the nature of the attitudes which the formulae are designed to release and to conceal. And what is most disheartening about it is not only the broad scale on which this poetry is being written, but also the easy way in which editors have been persuaded to accept it as the general climate of Australian creativity, and to accept the *Bulletin's* valuation of its own performers.

What is most disheartening is that it *is* the general climate, among writers and editors alike. We are in the middle of a period of Georgian poetry, a period of 'tough', jazzed-up Georgianism which has partly adapted itself to local conditions.

There would be some sense, too, in trying to find out what has brought us to this sorry pass. The first answer must be that Stewart and Judith Wright, in making their re-creation of reality graceful, have also succeeded in making it look easy. There is the trap, and it gapes for the older players as widely as for the younger. The kind of poem which these two so often write is short, composed of easily obtainable elements, and makes little stern demand on the sense of form. It requires neither stamina nor penetrating thought for its imitation. The same is true of the line which runs through Slessor to Mathew, Hart-Smith, and Nancy Keesing.

Added to this is the fact that the *Bulletin*, a weekly publication, is available to the young poet in a way that the quarterly journals cannot be. A poet still in his first formative period can get from Stewart a hearing, advice, rapid publication, and money — a combination of pleasant experiences which he would find it much harder to get anywhere else. This must be responsible for the number of 'discoveries' which the *Bulletin* has made over the past few years. Chief among these is Francis Webb, who for years published only in the *Bulletin*, but who has not permitted his quite individual talent to be encased in formulae of any kind. Yet the journal which 'discovers' a young poet has a good deal of influence over his literary production, whether or not the editor wishes to exercise it.

These factors almost certainly have something to do with the emergence of a *Bulletin* school of poetry; yet it would be absurd to maintain that they account for such an emergence. The period which I am considering is quite a short one, and obviously reasons of a much greater spiritual substance are needed to account for any literary trend over a short period.

The main reason, I think, lies in the adjacent fields of social forces and of literary continuity itself. The first may be summed up, doubtless in a far too simple way, by saying that there has been, since the war, a sort of hiatus in the movement of social forces in Australia, and that the poet, attempting to give full expression to his spiritual aspirations, can find no echo or image of them in the social aspirations of his people. The second is perhaps an even more complicated matter, and in any full study would have to be treated with the utmost delicacy. Yet here again we may say that there is a sort of hiatus. The ultimate literary influences on the poets with whom we are dealing are FitzGerald and Slessor; and FitzGerald's most influential book was published at about the same time as Slessor assumed his fifteen years' virtual silence. These two poets provided not only a technical guide, but also a guide to the attitudes which Australian poets might profitably adopt towards their country. But the gap between inspiration and emulation has been too big, and the impulse has become distorted and devitalized in the very attempt to reproduce it.

Judith Wright, McAuley, and Stewart are quite capable of discovering the Australian reality in their own way and in their
own terms, and at least two of them have learnt from the
older poets all they needed to learn. The rest of the *Bulletin*
school seem undecided under whose aegis their journalistic
gestures are to gain most attention; and so they huddle together for warmth, hoping that in the very acts of com-
panionship some magical power will emerge.

They are dazed by the size of the land, and the completeness of her geological history, just as they are bemused by the
objective life of her major city. If it is ever proper to prescribe
a way for poetry, I should say that they ought, rather, to be
amazed by her destiny, and should seek to make their poetry
a way of comprehending and recreating it.

Poetry and the 'New Christians'

SOME THREE or four years ago, the editors of the well-known American magazine *Partisan Review* conducted a symposium on the subject of the religious revival among intellectuals and writers. Though framed portentously and with every appearance of scientific completeness, their questions wore rather a wistful air; and they were almost reducible to a much simpler formula: 'How did this confounded thing happen to start? And is there much hope of it stopping by itself?'

To put the subject of their symposium in this way is not to gird at the editors themselves; for they had plainly decided that the 'revival', wherever it came from, had gone too far for comfort; it had to be reviewed; and they found it hard to keep the note of alarm out of their scientifically-pitched voices.

There were very few Christians among their famous contributors, yet nearly all of them agreed, tacitly at least, that the phenomenon which they were investigating was substantial enough to warrant investigation in terms of all the social sciences – anthropology, sociology, and psychology. Behind their studied gestures of agreement, behind their somewhat pretentious jargon, it is possible to see several dominant attitudes.

In the first place, there is the notion that the sociological approach to the phenomenon of widespread religious belief is the only one which is either relevant or meaningful. Religion is seen as something essentially divorced from the other activities of man, but also as something which is in no sense autotelic, which has no proper and autonomous sphere. It can be assessed only in terms of social causes and effects; it exists, like an exotic variant on a government health service, only to serve people conceived as social objects.

In the second place, there is a somewhat splenetic irritation at the fact that historical circumstances have made it necessary for them to study such a phenomenon at all. As it appears in their guarded comments, 'the religious revival' sounds as eccentric as a revival of the Guild system in industry; and the concern of intellectuals with it as annoying as an attempt to restore a Bronze Age civilization, rather than pleasing as raising from the dead the Lazarus of the modern world. In this way, six thousand years of incredibly rich and varied cultures are abolished with the easy assumption of a state of mind, and history becomes no more than an adjunct to, a means of reinforcing, the historical present.

In the third place, there is a feeling (and a quite genuine one) that, if the revival is to grow in its present form, it will mean a desertion of the humanist cause precisely at the moment when that cause is in greatest need of support and deepening.

It is this last feeling which most concerns me here; for I feel that, of the three unstated attitudes which give such plangency to the analysis of the *Partisan Review* contributors, this is the only one which has in it both factual substance and the presence of a truly civilized mentality. And it is also the most interesting, not only for the attitudes of the secularists themselves, but also for the stated or implied attitude of the Christians. Three or four of these contributed to the discussion. They were the only ones for whom the religious dimension had any compelling interest, for whom it was the one element which gave any reality to the discussion at all. Yet the remarkable thing about their contributions is the absence of any abiding joy in the facts which they interpret; there is in their essays a solitary note, a note of pathos and protestation mixed with the superiority; it is Kierkegaardian rather than communal, desolate rather than delighted, shot through with triumphant gloom rather than with the humanism which springs from and is irradiated with the liturgy.

I say all these things so bluntly not because I wish to undermine confidence in the objectivity of the non-believers, or to suggest a process of exorcism for the believers, but because what is implied quite strongly in the sociological and philosophical discussion achieves an aesthetic form in the writings of several modern poets who are either products of, or contributors to, the revival which we are considering.

It would be true to say that there *is* some sort of revival going on, at least in England and America. The past twenty years or so have seen an immense change in the emotional and intellectual climate of creative writing. The things which were orthodoxies as late as 1939 are orthodoxies no longer; and they are being not only driven out, but supplanted. This fact alone makes it necessary for writers, and particularly for those writers who are both Christian and humanist, to consider very closely just what is happening, precisely what the new orthodoxies amount to in terms which are human and humanist *because* they are Christian.

A sociological approach to the question is relevant, but it is relevant only if it is conceived to be one among other approaches. The few notes which follow may be considered hints towards the formulation of a sociology of the literature of the present moment. We can see several factors making for the revival of a religious world-view among intellectuals and writers; and it would be useful for a Christian to take note of those factors, if we regard them not as sufficient causes of the revival, but as occasions for it. To see the matter in this light is to see it only secondarily as a phenomenon which can be measured and tested and assigned explanations.

What has happened is undoubtedly that certain imaginative barriers to religious belief have been removed by the play of history itself. The materialist world-view tended to cramp the human personality – and, in particular, the creative imagination – by pretending to give too easy a satisfaction to its major aspirations. But every one of the natural goods which material-ism claimed to achieve for society has in fact receded farther into the future; wars, depressions, and the presence of such monstrosities of destruction as the great A- and H-bombs have delayed man's expectation of his ultimate fulfilment and, by dimming or destroying his exclusively social images of it, have released in him the possibilities of a wider imaginative grasp. The result is the breaking-down of barriers in the imagination itself, and the return of a more widespread religious faith.

It would be easy to call this a 'failure of nerve', a new *trahison des clercs;* but such statements are no more than catch-cries, unpropitiously buzzing one's own failure into ears which are sympathetic only because they too have heard the rumours of their failure. What the new intellectuals desire is not a source of facile consolation, as their critics so often suppose; it is a return to a sense of transcendence, a knowledge of God as acting obscurely in human affairs, while he transcends the form of those affairs; and it is, above all, a desire for a bond ('religio') with God on those terms of transcendence.

Yet it is also interesting to notice what form these aspirations have so far taken in practice. And here our delight begins to be modified, our sympathy with the 'religious' tempered by a feeling of mistrust. There is something incomplete, even defeatist, about the world-view of so many of them – something imperfectly Christian because imperfectly humanist, a lack of communal hope giving a strange twist to the movement of faith. If we regard the present situation as a transitional one, we may see certain psychological pressures acting in it, and tending to delay its proper growth. Many of the writers over the last twenty years of the nineteenth century and the first forty years of this were educated as Christians; and, in accepting the more narrow secularist philosophy which governed adult life, they came in their own adolescence and adulthood to regard this philosophy as a liberation from the things which had restricted them in childhood. The teaching of the Gospels and the memories of religious observance seemed to them an inevitable part of the world of reactionary parents, insensitive governesses, and the philistine public school. For the newer writers, the emphases are different. They reached adolescence during a major depression and adulthood during a series of wars which were as bitter in fact as they were ideological in nature – a series of wars which are still going on, and which become more hopeless with every outbreak of violence. These writers cannot help seeing themselves as separated from childhood by a slowly mounting wave of horror; the Gospels and religious observances of their childhood seem to them signs not of oppression but of the freedom of innocence – a 'green world' rather than a cage. It is proper to speak of these writers as converts, if one may speak of a conversion to a faith whose emotional weight derives mainly from a sort of desperate nostalgia.

I am not thinking so much of people like T. S. Eliot, Evelyn Waugh, or Graham Greene, but of the younger writers whom they, as well as the *Zeitgeist*, have influenced. Here, some knowledge of recent poetic movements is necessary if the facts are to have any meaning; and the anthologies are useful as examples of the state of mind in which these movements have crystallized.

The revolution which Ezra Pound and Eliot led against the Georgian universe was a revolution in content leading to a revolution in form. So was the revolution which Auden led (albeit with many gestures of sympathy and submission) against Eliot and Pound. The objection sustained by the 'poets of the thirties' to the methods of Eliot was primarily an objection to the lack of any positive view, which those methods were designed to conceal; 'The Waste Land', so the young writers averred, was useful as an analysis of capitalist society in decay, but it did not give man his due; modern man was revolutionary man, man realist. And although Auden himself was curtly informed by the Communists that he was not a Communist at all, but 'a bourgeois intellectual who had concluded an anarchist alliance with Communism', his revolt became the climate of a whole decade. The revolt against it came very quickly – came, in fact, with the emergence of George Barker and Dylan Thomas half-way through the thirties. It is with this emergence – or, rather, the climate to which it gave rise – that I am most concerned.

The poets who gathered round these two felt, and stated quite bluntly, that the Left-Wing poets and their collaborators drew on too narrow a range of experience for their conception of poetry and too shallow an exploration of the personality for its expression. In short, they did not recognize man as a total person, and so did not realize to the full his poetic possibilities. The proper models were no longer Byron and Shelley, Thomas Hardy and Eliot; they were the romantic disordering of the senses favoured by Rimbaud, the Surrealists' images of depth, the Jungian archetypes, Blake and Coleridge and a Donne far more Romantic than the tortured Classicist whom Eliot had restored to favour twenty years before.

The tendency was not yet religious – at least not explicitly so. Myth and its attendant colours of imagery were far more important than strictness of belief. The manifestos of neo-Romanticism can be found in three writers: in Francis Scarfe's *Auden and After*, a book which attempted to explain the rationale by which the younger poets were working; in *What is Apocalypse?* by Henry Treece, who led the more myth-conscious legions of the reformers; and in the works of Herbert Read, with their stress on anarchism and organic form.

It would do less than justice to the poetry of the early forties if one were to ignore the fact that they saw their doctrines as a prescription for something like a way of life, an implicit philosophy and politics as well as an approach to poetry. From the conception of poetry as an organic growth (as something resembling a plant or mineral organism far more than a building) it was an easy step to the conception of man as an organic being seeking his completion in an organic society, in which the instincts should give vitality to the works of reason.

But it was at this point that world castatrophe intervened. The pendulum was swinging rapidly in the direction of a natural religion; and just as it reached the height of its arc, historical circumstances pressed like an enormous hand to give it a still more violent momentum. The myths took on a religious flavour, and the somewhat hasty insistence on organic life became a climate of religiosity.

In England, Roy Campbell had long been a Catholic, and one who scorned climates of opinion as he would a plague; Auden went to America on the outbreak of war, and there announced himself an Anglican; Eliot had been developing a specifically Christian message for nearly fifteen years. These, however, are not the real makers of the new poetry. It is names like Norman Nicholson, Anne Ridler, John Heath-Stubbs, Kathleen Raine, which begin to arrest our eyes in the anthologies and reviews. And sounding behind them all like a slightly brassy trumpet canters the prophetic voice of Edith Sitwell.

An age which claims Dr Sitwell as a great poet may be prepared to admit that she is also a representative one; and, on the surface, she seems to have a good deal to say to us in our perplexity:

> The Catastrophes with veils and trains drift by,
> And I to my heart, disastrous Comet, cry
> 'Red heart, my Lucifer, how fallen art thou,
> And lightless, I!'
> The dresses sweep the dust of mortality
> And roll the burden of Atlas' woe, changed to a stone
> Up to the benches where the beggars sway—
> Their souls alone as on the Judgment Day—
> In their Valley of the myriad Dry Bones under world-tall houses.
> Then with a noise as if in the thunders of the Dark
> All sins, griefs, aberrations of the world rolled to confess,

Those myriad Dry Bones rose to testify:
'See her, the Pillar of Fire'!
The aeons of Cold
And all the deaths that Adam has endured
Since the first death, can not outfreeze our night.
And where is the fire of love that will warm our hands?
There is only this conflagration
Of all the sins of the world!

It does not require a line-to-line analysis to show that, if this
is prophecy, it is a prophecy startlingly less explicit and particu-
larized than we should like. It is frustrating to be told something
important about our fate, and yet to be told it in such a way that
the very means of its expression prevent us from discovering
what it is. This passage is all violent colour, Old Testament
echoes, boring rhythmical changes, and vague oratorical gesture;
and it seems to have no other purpose than to let us know that
the world is done for, that it has been overtaken (whether
blessedly or not, we are not informed) by its final cataclysm.
Nearly all Dr Sitwell's recent poems are in fact variations on
the one poem; yet she never really tells us what attitude she is
adopting to the events she purports to be chronicling. Her God is
certainly no lover of mankind; if any God is discernible at all
in the centre of her riotous oratory is is such a God as might be
conceived by a witless and terrified Job, who did not know what
was happening or why, but who knew only that he was in for it.
But Dr Sitwell sets an example which, happily, has seldom
been followed – at least in kind. Other poets are more interested
in making some human sense of their present predicament.
What that sense amounts to in terms of poetry is another matter.
George Barker, for example, attempts to locate a meaning by
using a sort of terrified blasphemy:

Incubus. Anaesthetist with glory in a bag,
Foreman with a sweatbox and a whip. Asphyxiator
Of the ecstatic. Sergeant with a grudge
Against the lost lovers in the park of creation,
Fiend behind the fiend behind the fiend behind the
Friend. Mastodon with mastery, monster with an ache
At the tooth of the ego, the dead drunk judge:
Wheresoever Thou art our agony will find Thee
Enthroned on the darkest altar of our heartbreak
Perfect. Beast, brute, bastard. O dog my God!

This has a certain sincerity, and the laughter which it arouses should be a sympathetic one. Yet the religious conception which it embodies has something in common with that of Dr Sitwell. Man is, in some unspecified way, a sinner, and so deserves to be robbed of his hope, even of his positive faith, by a torturing God. There is little more for the poet to say than to announce the fact.

Hope may be defined as faith made positive and active in the fires of charity, and directed to man's threefold source of vision – to God, to his fellow-men, and to the material creation. The more orthodox poets adopt an attitude to experience which is in some respects opposed to those of Barker and Dr Sitwell; and we might hope, by analysing the positive or negative nature of that attitude, to hint at the quality of faith (poetic as well as religious) which gives rise to it.

Norman Nicholson and Anne Ridler are in some sense disciples of Eliot. Their view of man and his history is soundly based on the liturgy, and it finds its poetic expression through a reliance on the ordinary, day-to-day experiences of men and women. It is an unpretentious minor poetry; and yet it is not quite so unpretentious as it pretends to be. For one thing, it does purport to establish a Christian sanity in the midst of the insane world; and one gains the uneasy feeling that it does so largely by discounting or ignoring the world of men, and considering Christianity as something special, something additional to experience, a pleasant yet somehow necessary patina on the contours of living:

> This is the day the air has eyes,
> And the Devil falls like hail
> From the bright and thundering skies,
> And soaks into soil and rock,
> And the bad blood rises in nettle and dock,
> And toadstools burst like boils between the toes of the trees.
>
> The war that began in heaven still goes on.
> Thorn trees twist like spears,
> The owl haunts the grain,
> The coursed rabbit weeps icicles of tears;
> But the feathers of the clouds foretell
> St. Michael's victory in the purged and praising rain.

It is a personal and revealing way of looking at the landscape of a winter's day; yet, as it is presented here, it does not ring true. Man, Nicholson's full Christian man, is too much an observer of life, looking on at the battle between Good and Evil as though it were something quite outside himself. It is an approach which excludes too much, and which excludes in especial man immersed in his society. This battle could be terminated abruptly for good or ill, and we hardly know it. The mood is one of awareness, but of awareness from outside life, with a suggestion about it of quietism and passive surrender to God conceived as fate. Though offered with devotion and a certain love, this attitude of certain orthodox Christians is too limited, too much tinged with an anti-humanist sadness, a sad carnality, for us to be entirely easy about it.

No doubt, in these two halves of the modern poetic personality, grappling with religious realities, we are simply seeing shock acting on the one hand as an anaesthetic, and on the other as an incitement to hysteria. No doubt, too, it will all pass away; but in the meantime a whole culture is being influenced. Hysteria has become one orthodoxy, religious quietism another. And poetry as an art is becoming more and more a matter of the replacement of metaphor and graceful statement by a series of disconnected conceits. Almost everyone seems to be affected by it. It is true that more than half of the few good poets still writing are Christians; there are Gascoyne and Watkins in Britain, Robert Lowell and Tate in the United States. And the goodness of their work can not be entirely divorced from the fact that their Christianity is also a humanism, an attempt to show human society, with all its aspirations and failures, its hopes and fears, as the incarnation of certain spiritual realities which of their nature transcend the realities in which they are incarnated. Such an attempt is not theological, but poetic; or rather, it gains its logical meaning only through first being poetry. Even so, in the present circumstances of our world, it seems to be able to attain its ultimate human relevance only at the cost of a temporary withdrawal into the regions of myth and colour, where indirectness is king.

Robert Lowell, for example, has a magnificent talent, which is seldom used to the full. His vision is said to be basically

religious and even liturgical; yet the emotions in which it is
expressed are too often the dour pessimism of his puritan fore-
bears. This is an unpleasant heritage for any modern poet to
carry, and in exchanging it for Catholicism Lowell does not seem
to have gained any great joy in the buying of his birthright. God
and the Saints appear not as steady lights to which the human
condition tends, but as a series of agonizing flashes in Lowell's
own experience, to be ultimately dissolved in the stormy and
penitential flux of life. Yet they do not incite either to the
hysteria of dread or to a mystic smugness. As elements in the
poetry they may be imperfectly assimilated, but they are always
relevant; and in consequence man's fate is always noble as it
is always, in some sense, assured.

Vernon Watkins too is conscious of the Incarnation in the
only way in which a poet can be conscious of it : as transforming
the quality of the mind and senses themselves. For him, as for
Allen Tate, 'religious poetry' is not a special genre, because
religion is not a special part of life; Christian life is the whole of
life transformed, and Christian poetry is not poetry about Christ,
no matter under what guise he is conceived, but an attitude of
mind which sees the whole world at once re-ordered and transformed in Christ. Consequently, his lyric 'Indolence' is quite as
'religious' as his more dogmatic and expository poems :

> Count up those books whose pages you have read
> Moulded by water. Wasps this paper made.
> Come. You have taken tribute from the dead.
> Your tribute to the quick must now be paid.
>
> What lovelier tribute than to rest your head
> Beneath this birchtree which is bound to fade?
> And watch the branches quivering by a thread
> Beyond interpretation of the shade.

A hostile critic might well say that here is quietism pure and
simple; yet the movement of the poetry itself is not quietist. On
the contrary, it is vibrant with spiritual assurance, a set of
reverberations which show how active is the sensibility behind
it. This not the poetry of a man who is overcome by dread or
sloth; it is the poetry of a man who says : 'God can fill both my
soul and my body with life that is the fruit of love. Yet man is

sick and suffering from the world; let me go to him through my
poetry, for poetry is the only means I have.'

Such confidence, not in oneself, but in one's art and its sources,
is to be found too in the fiercer poetry of David Gascoyne; for
him, hatred and oppression are an affront to the image of Christ
which exists in all men. This is the final rage of humanism:

> Behind His lolling head the sky
> Glares like a fiery cataract
> Red with the murders of two thousand years
> Committed in His name and by
> Crusaders, Christian warriors
> Defending faith and property.
>
> Amid the plain beneath His transfixed hands,
> Exuding darkness as indelible
> As guilty stains, fanned by funereal
> And lurid airs, besieged by drifting sands
> And clefted landslides our about-to-be
> Bombed and abandoned cities stand.
>
> He who wept for Jerusalem
> Now sees his prophecy extend
> Across the greatest cities of the world,
> A guilty panic reason cannot stem
> Rising to raze them all as He foretold;
> And He must watch the drama to the end.

Of these poets, some exert a baneful influence, based on a
false sense of their importance and even on a misunderstanding
of their basic attitudes; the 'explosive image' which was thought
to be so healthy a force in modern poetry is used here in
the interests of an anti-humanist attitude which at the same
time it seeks to conceal. The dominant note is one of a moral
and spiritual vertigo barely kept under control by its images
and conceits. Others of them are genuine poets, yet even in their
work the central ideas are of disorder and a rich confusion; there
are very few images of growth or, indeed, of any strength
except that of Samson, reducing to ruins a dead and blas-
phemous temple. A poetry which proclaims its own religious
nature cannot be fully representative of a culture and a people
which make no such claim, even though it may be held to foreshadow a communal change in heart of that people. But that is
not the most worrying thing; one is worried, rather, by a

religious poetry which is either fulsome or withdrawn, which hymns the Incarnation in images of death rather than of life, and which announces for man a destiny not so much terrible as lost in an ever-darkening future. One does not expect a poetry which carries cheerful messages. One expects that any poetic climate which claims to be Christian should purge itself of dead myths and should reflect or enact the vibrant quality of a Christian life in all its moods. And it is precisely this which is least in evidence.

The situation is different in Australia; it is also, perhaps, more genuinely hopeful. Australian poets are, for the most part, living on the emotional capital of an outlook which we might call the 'humanism of pioneers'. So far as we can see, the country herself is not yet fully explored and unselfconsciously·present to the poetic mind, and a good deal of our modern poetry is an attempt to find a means of making her fully present. Yet over the past twenty years the dramatic and naturalistic view of man as engaged in a morally neutral struggle against natural forces has begun to change. Poets *are* beginning to write about society, and are seeking myths by which to reveal the essential nature of the bonds between men. It follows that a more integral and a more Christian humanism is beginning to supplant the humanism centred on a bushman hero. Even so, the process is slow. Christian poets, such as Picot or James McAuley, are still slightly apart from the tradition of our poetry as a whole — which may be a reason why McAuley, in particular, is not given his proper recognition by Australian critics. In the work of Francis Webb — another Catholic — the religious dimension is always there, but it tends to be obscured *as statement* by the extraordinary density of his images.

For our best poets man, whether or not he is seen as the servant and co-adjutor of God, is the central fact of experience. So far, he has been dwarfed by the size of the country, but he is still central to her. The minor poets are not here in question, for most of them are four or five decades behind the development of Australia herself. For the others, man is a being whose life is characterized by the struggle to love, and to realize his hope and courage in creative action; for such poets as McAuley, Slessor, and Judith Wright, this struggle is reflected in their efforts to attain a poetic form in which to achieve their dominant images. And love, secular and sacred, is a key word. Even in the work of Judith Wright, a non-Christian poet, it has the breadth and ambience of a myth which is not arbitrary but wholly satisfying:

> A god has chosen to be shaped in flesh.
> He has put on the garment of the world.
> A blind and sucking faith, a huddled worm,
> he crouches there until his time shall come,
> all the dimensions of his glory furled
> into the blood and clay of the night's womb.
> Eternity is locked in time and form.
>
> Within those mole-dark corridors of earth
> how can his love be born and how unfold?
> Eternal knowledge in an atom's span
> is bound by its own strength with its own chain.
> The nerve is dull, the eyes are stopped with mould,
> the flesh is slave of accident or pain.
> Sunk in his brittle prison-cell of mud
> the god who once chose to become a man
> is now a man who must become a god.

The poem has the simple and challenging title of 'Myth'; yet it is characteristic, in its grasp of the factual and earthy, of the religious note which is coming into our poetry. The Incarnation is seen under its human rather than under its divine and redemptive aspects. This fact alone testifies to the 'immanentist' nature of Australian thinking about religion at the same time as it guarantees that the images will be hopeful, strong, and full of growth. For Gascoyne, Christ is man suffering; for Miss Wright, He is man aspiring. The difference is instructive; and it should be stressed that it is a difference between two good poets of separate cultures. Some people may prefer to say that the general difference is one between two different stages of decay in the one culture; to say so is to renounce the very hope whose desirability I have been stressing, and to give a radically different analysis from the one I have been giving. A hope for religion is bound up with a hope for humanity, and the humanist hope rests ultimately in Christ as the source of growth. In McAuley's 'The Incarnation of Sirius', World War II is accompanied by a war in the whole cosmic order, symbolized by the organized revolt of the stars and planets. Not only that: the two revolts against order are mutually dependent, inter-active. His later poetry, as in the lovely 'Canticle', presents Christian love as the meaning of sexual love, Agape as the force behind Eros. R. D. FitzGerald shares the vision neither of Miss Wright nor of McAuley; but his poetry is one long plea for informed courage in the face of an incomprehensible destiny.

All these emphases are significant; and their social and cultural occasions are too obvious to mention. It is not that Australian poets are individually better as poets than their English and American counterparts. The general climate here is, however, more conducive to a poetic expansion and strengthening than the climate in most other countries. It is true that Australia as a land has not yet suffered the purgation of fire; and it may be equally true that she will not develop a truly religious poetry until she has done so. On the other hand, I see no reason for assuming the truth of this latter proposition. As the world shrinks in space, we are going to be more deeply and continuously influenced by poetic developments overseas than we have so far. And many things in their convergence persuade me that we are in for a period in which an attempt will be made to expand humanism by drawing out in poetry its full religious significance. This attempt will probably breed its own reaction in the shape of a militant paganism offering its system of myths as an alternative to Christianity. This, however, should not dismay us; the full vision of man and his destiny on the earth is made possible only through struggle. While the basis of that struggle is being laid, it is very important for secularists to understand that the 'religious revival' which so alarms them is not an organized backward movement in the name of obscurantism; and it is equally important for Christians to realize that in none of the three countries which I have mentioned is there being produced an adequate image of the Incarnation which some men profess and to which all unknowingly aspire.

Helicon as Jordan

IN THAT BRILLIANT yet confusing book, *The Creative Element*, Stephen Spender makes one remark which is most revealing; and it is all the more revealing in that it is a remark made more or less casually:

> The 'creative element' has been the amazing release of individual vision *without any allegiance to society*, which allowed writers to think that in their art they were exploring primal values of aesthetic experience. [It is a] faith in the absoluteness of the poetic image.

Art, not God, is the transcendent principle before which men must bow; but it is a transcendence which is somehow part of the very personality of each great writer, a touchstone which, as his art develops, comes to be the principle of his life as well. It is the hidden life-spring of the individual's action, his means of creating his own divinity. Life is not subordinate to art; art *is* life.

We cannot avoid the conclusion, in facing these claims, that art *as a process* is seen to derive its emotional force from feeding on its own vitals. In the process, of course, it exhausts its own resources, for the human being – even the artist – is not possessed of a liver which is perpetually renewable. At this point, it is interesting to note that the position which Spender analyses also involves a sort of social Manichæism. Society itself, and not some social conditions, is seen as the 'destructive element'; genius does well, therefore, to move outside society, and in some sense in opposition to it.

Here is the Arnoldian thesis leading, if not to madness, at least to fatty degeneration of the heart; here is a modern *'credo quia impossibile'*. It is as though society existed outside human beings, and did not impregnate them with its values. But the voice which announces this gospel is all the more important in that it is fully articulate and even, at a profound level, representative of one of the great world-views of our time. Rimbaud and Rilke, Kafka and Yeats – all are mobilized to sing Alleluia before

93

the fluid God of an asocial aesthetic. They set up 'works which are substitute spiritual institutions'; and these are valuable not so much as persuasive answers by which all men can live but as signs of the 'disappearance of values'. If this were all that was claimed for them, we might give ready assent. But their pretension to be 'substitute spiritual institutions' remains; and it cannot be allowed.

These claims are valuable, however, as an indication of the European dilemma, which may shortly (though it has not yet) become the dilemma of creative writers in Australia. The English literary world at the moment gives evidence of a vitality which has been seriously impaired.[1] The usual reasons are given for this: an uninformed public, lack of patronage, a partisan criticism, and 'ivory towerism'; but they will hardly convince any informed observer that they are in themselves a sufficient explanation. What has happened, I think, is that the nature of poetry itself has come to be conceived in a light dangerous to its own future development. It has become, broadly speaking, a way of exploring one's own mental and emotional states under cover of certain largely conventional myths or objective correlatives, and at the same time a desperate expedient for obtaining some order in a chaotic world. It is being seen more and more as a metaphysic rather than an art.

Of course, poetry is always in some sense a voyage of discovery; in the very process of creation, the poet discovers and strengthens ties between himself and the various aspects of external reality; and he expresses the existence and meaning of those ties at the moment of their fullest realization. Of course it works best in a society which is philosophically and culturally settled. The accepted concepts of a culture become, through being used as images by successive artists and thinkers, the central peaks of meaning around which individual experiences tend to group themselves, and with reference to which they take their appropriate form. So much can be assumed, and can give richness and point to whatever else is discovered in the individual consciousness. It is not the insistence on discovery which alarms us at the present moment, but the thing which is to be discovered, and

---

[1] For the purposes of this essay the statement must remain without demonstration by an appeal to the works of individual writers.

which is so important that it warrants a total withdrawal from society in order to discover it.

The *Zeitgeist,* that ambiguous and probably non-existent monster, has wrought so powerfully on the artist's imagination that he has allowed it to grab him by the short hairs. The great writers of this century have been all too concerned with themselves as the *source* of their own work. Virginia Woolf and Rilke are obvious examples of the self-renewing ego; but the matter begins to appear serious and of general import when we find that we can apply the same judgment to Yeats and Joyce. Much as I admire him, I cannot see Joyce's last work as anything but a staggering hoax which ended by hoaxing its author. And the more powerful of the last poems of Yeats derive much of their anguish from an attempt to re-create the world in terms of his own sexual aspiration. These are men who, in seeking to find an ultimate meaning in the very processes of art, succeeded in losing a large part of the meaning which they had previously discovered. And three of the four are great artists; the loss has been greater since their deaths. An age which does not protest against the exaltation of Christopher Fry to the status of a great artist is heading for a state in which art becomes lost in entertainment: and in an entertainment all the more deceptive in that it presides, cheerfully enough, over the consummation of the marriage between moral uplift and obscurity.

English poetry now gets from outside itself no intellectual vitality, no urge to explore the external world and to uncover its real meaning; it gets these stabilizing impulses neither from the processes of society itself nor from the ideas which underlie society and which in certain ways become part of social living. In these circumstances, it is inevitable that, if poetry is to have any sustained vitality at all, it should attempt to gain such vitality from becoming a substitute for metaphysics, a 'spiritual' order in the mind and achieved by the mind alone, to which, however, the emotions can give assent and for which they are, indeed, partly responsible. We ought not to be surprised therefore by the presence of a tendency to etherialize the poetic impulse by withdrawing it from the full and ordered operation of the senses.

In such a dilemma, which the younger poets at least feel

keenly, there will be recourse to a series of desperate expedients
for achieving the vitality which poets cannot find in society, and
with which, by reason of their own feeble commitment, they
cannot endow society. But these expedients will, for the most
part, remain external to the poetic impulse itself. One has only
to think of the disintegration caused by political comment in the
work of Jack Lindsay, Edgell Rickword, and Spender; one can
readily see the indecisiveness coming from the use of psychological theories – Auden's much-loved Homer Lane, and the
devotion of the 'Apocalypse' to the theories of Freud and Jung;
above all, one is struck by the rapidity with which the dilemma
felt by the poets drove them to seek a solution in a new attitude
to imagery, and by the equal rapidity with which that imagery
let them down.

   This, I think, is an important point, and I am sorry that I
cannot here give it the scholarly attention which it deserves. It
must be stressed that the poetic developments of the past twenty
years are not due to a wanton carelessness about form; nor are
they due, however, to an experimental spirit conducting its experiments in a vacuum. Much of the talk which goes on in the
pages of the advanced reviews may be pretentious, and it may be
self-deception; but it is self-deception in a cause greater than that
of mere talking. It arises, in short, from a failure to understand
what poetry can do, and what it cannot do. It is an attempt,
noble yet misguided, to construct a universe of the imagination
which shall be both organic and autonomous, born of man yet
transcendent and in some sense preternatural.

   The reliance on 'the explosive image', the greedy capitalizing
on the last will and testament of the Surrealists, the use of names
like 'Apocalypse', are merely aids to the formation of the poet's
new universe. That universe itself rests on an almost vegetative
use of myth and religion. Its main prophet is Dylan Thomas
who, had he lived, might have discovered the reasons which
govern the possession of genius:

> The force that through the green fuse drives the flower
> Drives my green age; that blasts the roots of trees
> Is my destroyer.
> And I am dumb to tell the crooked rose
> My youth is bent by the same wintry fever.

The force that drives the water through the rocks
Drives my red blood; that dries the mouthing streams
Turns mine to wax.
And I am dumb to mouth unto my veins
How at the mountain spring the same mouth sucks.

This is a poetry both formed and forceful. Yet as the poem
proceeds, what had begun as a *comparison* between man's fate of
dumb despair and the acquiescence of natural forces in their own
destruction becomes an *identification* of two states – the human
and the sub-human. The first comes to be imaginatively realized,
because it is seen, in terms of the second.

The point I am trying to make is one which curiously evades
exact statement. Yet we may see in the work of Thomas, Hendry,
W. S. Graham and Tom Scott, as of many other writers, something of an attempt to submerge themselves in, to become identified with, a universe which is primarily one of vegetative growth.
Far too many of them seem to think not only of human experience but also of social processes in images drawn from biology
and botany, and sealed with a little psychology. It is not so much
anthropomorphism as its opposite, a vegetative mysticism; and it
is not entirely to be rejected, for it has undoubtedly enriched the
poetic possibilities of the language. Yet as a solution to the mystery of man's place in the modern world, it is eccentric and even
a little monstrous – a metaphysic of the belly and of the lower
members.

And it has, of course, done nothing to increase or deepen the
social relevance of poetry. Perhaps one is foolish to expect that
it should. But in the long run, it cannot do much either to im-
prove the poetry itself; and it cannot help, I think, in encouraging (where it does not create) the 'dissociation of sensibility' so
typical of our time.

I do not wish to insist that most of the recent English poets are
animists; the sub-human mysticism in which such poets as
Thomas seek the sources of human life is only one of the ex-
tremes – and perhaps the most exciting one – to which the
general imagination is driven. There are, after all, three other
points of the imaginative compass to be taken into account; and
if Thomas represents a true North, such poets as Empson and
Ronald Bottrall, with their wry intellectuality, may be regarded
as providing a somewhat dowdy South. But the work of Empson

and Bottrall shows, in its very phrasing, an attempt to evade, rather than to transcend, the challenge of the age. They seek to accomplish by complexity of allusion and variations in 'civilized tone' what the more vital poets find in the construction of a self-contained world more primitive than that in which most of us live; and they are certainly the less important, as they are the less representative voice.

Thomas and the 'Apocalypse' take Rilke and Rimbaud to a logical conclusion; they express as a total view of life what is merely hinted at or confused in the work of other schools. And they prefer a complete answer to an expansive and satisfying one. They are willing to exclude many elements of living and thought if, in the process of exclusion, they can generate a world which 'owes no allegiances' and which is sufficiently rich in emotional appeal to suggest its own enormous significance, without ever making that significance clear. The result is an enriching – an enriching not of the understanding but of the language. To this extent, it is a limited and limiting poetry. And as a symptom of a general cultural state, it has about it something of neurosis. The desire for completeness at the expense of truth and human sympathy is a typically neurotic device for concealing from oneself the less pleasant aspects of one's place in society.

There seems, at least in England, neither a current of ideas nor a set of social circumstances which can engage sensibility, mind, and will together in the developing act of poetry. Rather, such a fusion is impossible except through extraordinary struggle on the part of the poet. It is significant that Yeats needed a new, and in some sense bogus, cosmogony before he could pose his experience to himself in the most appropriately dramatic terms. The issue which he faced with such magnificent resourcefulness is precisely the one to which Thomas turns with a kit of burglar's tools, and which the Sitwells, either with witty inconsequence or with prophetic pretentiousness, refuse to face at all: it is the issue of the place of the religious consciousness in a world which rejects all transcendent values. And it is the existence of this issue which will probably lead posterity to see the failure of Hart Crane and Auden, while it will certainly qualify the present admiration for T. S. Eliot.

The issue has not really been faced in Australia; the fact that it has not is probably a reason for the dowdiness and lack of urgency in most of our poetry; but since it is not yet seen as a real creative problem, its existence has not yet become a source of confusion, still less of ineptitude. No doubt the reasons for this do no particular credit to Australian poets. And the social pressures behind it make it readily explicable.

In this country, society and the premises on which society is founded still allow poets to explore the external world in terms of man's real hopes and fears. Australian poetry has, for sixty years, been a way of investigating the Australian environment under various of its aspects, and of doing so in terms which maintain a necessary balance between man and nature, even while it stresses the reciprocity between them. I mentioned the variety of aspects under which the land has been approached. It is also true that there has been a steady advance in the completeness with which each aspect has come to be assumed into the poetic consciousness, and in the complexity to which the growth in assimilation has given rise. Our early poetry represented a discovery of the country as an historical fact; from there, we had a discovery of her as landscape, of her characteristic shapes and colours forming a natural palette for the expression of recurring human feelings. The general run of our poets are still in this second stage of adaptation; the best writers, among them Slessor, Judith Wright, McAuley and Hope, have triumphantly surpassed it. Their discovery has been directed to the ritual significance of the land; and, naturally enough, it has proceeded side by side with the poems of mental adventure written by Robert FitzGerald and Douglas Stewart and Francis Webb, poems in which we find an emphasis on human characterization demanding and finding its complement in an emphasis on *character*, forcefulness and purpose, in the land itself. A rich ritualism of description has its complement in a mood of personification, of giantism, very different from the pallid and conventional personification achieved by the Anglicizers of the nineteenth century.

Now, the main facts about the landscape of the country have been set down; its characteristic shapes and colours are part of the poet's sensibility. Any movement in the direction of an open 'nativism', of Australianism, must now appear not only as an anachronism but also as a failure of poetic interest and taste. But it is at this point that the greatest challenge is thrown out to us by the land herself; only in two or three instances have the poets got down to dealing with Australian society as such. One task at least is being undertaken with an adequate sense of purpose; that is the task of consolidating the common ideas and aspirations which as a community we have already had. But each writer must ask himself and his fellows: 'In what terms are we to continue to see Australia and our commitment to her?' There is an increasing, though scarcely articulate feeling that these terms should be at once social and religious, or at the very least social and mythical. McAuley, Judith Wright, and Webb are already assuming the responsibilities of leadership – responsibilities which, until very recently, had been ably shouldered by FitzGerald, Slessor and one or two others.

The true native note is no longer struck in the Jindyworobak coo-ee, but in the graceful tunings-up of McAuley's 'Celebration of Love,' or in Judith Wright's exploratory 'The Harp and the King', published side by side with an excellent article on her work by R. F. Brissenden:[2]

> I sing the praise of time and of the rain –
> the word creation speaks.
> Four elements are locked in time;
> the sign that makes them fertile is the seed,
> and this outlasts all death and springs again,
> the running water of the harp-notes cried.
>
> But the old king sighed obstinately
> How can that comfort me?
> Night and the terror of the soul come on,
> and out of me both water and seed have gone.
> What other generation shall I see?
> But make me trust my failure and my fall,
> said the sad king, since these are now my all.
>
> I sing the praise of time, the harp replied.
> In time we fail, alone with hours and tears,
> ruin our followers and traduce our cause,
> and give our love its last and fatal hurt.
> In time we fail and fall.
> In time the company even of God withdraws
> and we are left with our own murderous heart.

It is not that these poets lack tension, but that the tension in the soul is for the most part an ordered one, drawing stability and sap from a world which it would be churlish to reject. It is a world, too, in which the human person can see himself as a separate and distinct entity; neither the world nor the ego is treated as a substitute for the other. There is no question of the potentialities of the imagination being arbitrarily limited by a kind of identification of the two which really forbids them to co-operate in the act of creation. There is, on the contrary, that reciprocity which alone is certain strength.

It may be thought an intolerable paradox that the less cultured and resonant society should, in one important aspect of its poetry, surpass the more cultured society. One might think that the existence in England of a greater complexity of experience and of more stirring and rapidly-changing events would provide English poets with a wider and richer range of subject-matter. In point of fact, however, nearly every European poet today has difficulty in finding a subject-matter which is both relevant to himself as a person and capable of a consistent expansion through consistent use; he has difficulty, that is, in finding his own *theme*. As I have said, society itself does not provide any stimulus to the discovery of such a subject-matter; and very few poets have a faith wide and deep enough to provide a framework within which mind and sensibility together may develop, and which will help them to select things and events with an adequate sense of their significance. Instead of a framework of this kind, many of them have provided themselves with a view of poetry which is essentially solipsistic. The best English poetry has a surface more suggestive than its Australian counterpart; but the Australian lack of sophistication has as its most fortunate companion a salutary lack of the narcissism which sophistication is liable to breed. Therein lies its strength; a strength which, however, must be temporary unless we are capable of grasping the possibilities which it presents to us.

The general comparison may perhaps be made by comparing the English and Australian uses of *time* as part of the myths by which they are severally attempting to live. Even the mention

2 *Meanjin*, Spring 1953, no. 54, vol. xii, number 3, pp. 250, 255.

of such a theme opens up enormous possibilities for analysis and comment; yet it should be possible to make a few brief notations serve the purpose of indicating those possibilities, without in any way exhausting or distorting them. Time (spelt often with a capital) is at once the bugbear and the prized talisman of poetry in every country. The very word has the hypnotic qualities of a snake swaying in front of that mongoose, the modern poet. A recent article in *Perspectives* shows decisively to what extent Virginia Woolf's experiments with form were affected by Bergson's view of time; the montage practised by Apollinaire was a way of attempting to release the variegated life of the modern world from the necessities imposed on it by its existence in time and in a pattern of cause and effect; Joyce and Faulkner both use time as an infinitely malleable element in which events can be made to adopt their full symbolic significance. In all of these writers, the uses of time are genuinely experimental and creative; they represent an attempt to get into art as much as possible of the pattern of life and of the hidden significance of its detail. Yet in the work of each of them, time is beginning faintly to appear not as a friend but as an enemy, an agent of dissolution and a weapon for separating human lives within the one community.

In the work of later writers, time's metamorphosis from Dr Jekyll to Mr Hyde has become more noticeable. Almost under our gaze, the bestial hair sprouts on the cheeks, and teeth take on the sharpness of fangs. Time is no longer sequence, but the moment of impending death; and the poetry of the younger writers becomes, in large measure, a way of evading this realization by constructing a world which is independent of time, and which may be held to pre-date human consciousness; for the human is the only form of consciousness in which time may be directly apprehended as an enemy.

Examples could be given, but they would prove nothing; the generalization which I am making is too wide – though it would be proper to insist that I do not intend it to be an all-inclusive one. It might be instructive, however, to point out a difference between the use of shifting changes of view in Joyce's *Ulysses* and a similar device in Sartre's *The Reprieve*.

In the former, each dislocation of the temporal sequence serves to add to our sense that one complete action is being presented, and that it has an extremely rich pattern of cross-references which help to unify it. In the latter, it is used ironically to show how ineluctably isolated each human action is at a given moment; it is a way of stressing the essential boredom of being a person.

The poets are even more securely gripped by this pre-occupation; the more securely in having less artistic justification than Sartre for possessing it at all. It often seems that words such as 'time' and 'history' are simply their favourite abstract nouns, for which, by a change in taste, others could be substituted. But to go by the appearance would be to do less than justice to the psychological reality which enforces it as a habit of diction. There is, in fact, a deep and often impotent sense of being caught up in the path of an impending doom, an existential apprehension full of fear and oppression, a keen and ever-present realization of the possibility that the self may suddenly disintegrate or dissolve under the pressure of history. The here and now of the seeing self is ·the only reality, and it is the most insecure of all realities.

Among the Australian poets, too, there is a pre-occupation with time; though among them the terms 'time' and 'history' seem to be virtually interchangeable. The awareness itself is more detached and general; it is not that time is less keenly felt or perceived, but that it is perceived from a different perspective, a different and more encouraging distance. It is seen not so much as the immediate agent of the self's dissolution but as a force affecting movements, cultural activities, family trees – all realities which may be conceived as contributing to the life of the self and yet standing, in some sense, outside it.

The emotion, then, is not so clearly agonized; but it provides a wider context. There *is*, it is true, a certain anguish in Slessor, McAuley, and Judith Wright, but its root is in other causes, and the impatience with time is only one of its expressions. Australia is (of course) isolated from those social cataclysms which have induced in the European poet so despairing a view of his function. Her poets are still savouring the comparatively new freshness and size of the land, and spinning myths out of their delight; and they are still sufficiently part of the normal life of the Australian people to feel that poetry – their poetry – has the task of expressing and re-presenting to that people the aspirations of which they themselves are scarcely aware. Poetry in Australia still wears the air – becoming a little rarefied now – of a social function. While it retains anything at all of that air it cannot readily be used as a metaphysical absolute, a 'substitute spiritual institution'.

Another factor making for the stability of Australian poetry is the character of the country itself. Eternity for us is not enshrined in cultural and social institutions, and so is not seen as belonging exclusively to man. Rather, eternity is presented to our imaginations by the bush and the plains, the great incalculable heaps of rock and tree which we call mountains, and the sea which both joins us to and separates us from the European sources of our culture. In older cultures, eternity is enshrined in buildings, cultural habits, and traits of behaviour – all leading to a belief in social permanence. The agonized pre-occupation with time as a destructive force is a sure sign that those institutions are being shaken, are having their eternity drained from them. It could hardly be otherwise; and the effort of spiritual adjustment which it enforces on creative artists could hardly help proving, at least in most instances, one difficult to sustain. Time becomes a tyrant when eternity is attributed to things which are not really capable of bearing the attribution; and it becomes a nausea when those things are no longer stable enough to provide even a focus for man's aspirations in time.

Pick up any English anthology of the present day, and you pick up a record of the various attempts to escape the reality of time while crowning its bust with laurel. Quite at random, I open the book at J. F. Hendry's 'Elegy No. 5', and the hand of the poet begins immediately to twitch away the withered leaves:

> Spider of patience, I try to find you in a tangle
> Of memories, hidden perhaps like an anemone.
> I too conjure you up through the ganglia
> Of nerves' fear; and, more than sick money,
> Child, or science, seek through the brain's storm
> Two flowers I dropped, your face and form.

Smile your lovely smile upon my impudence!
Let your white laughter of teeth see my sorrow
Tremble through the leaves of your blind fingers!
All my being is an animal in anger
And in pain, confounded by your absence.
Birds, beasts and flowers know nothing of tomorrow

And yet, O more than bird's eye, beast's foot or the tense
Trumpet of an ear of flowers I miss you, dear one, now.

No experience gives certainty of anything but the horrors of
time exacting its tribute of fascinated pre-occupation. For
Slessor, on the other hand, time is 'the flood that does not flow',
a principle of movement and of salutary change which, due to
an extraordinary circumstance, has ceased to act out its nature.
Yet there is no suggestion that time is really and inescapably
like that, but rather that the poet's mind has temporarily caused
it to appear like that.

In this respect, as in others, the Australian poets do not generally use their art as a means of direct self-analysis, or of discovering the essence of their individual selves. The discovery which is
made is always of a link between the self and the social facts
which reflect and modify it. There is a perennial reliance on
themes of ancestry, and of the individual inheriting from the
past a communal life. The explorations in verse of Australian
history are already bearing rich fruit; Captain Cook has left
more than his blind henchman, Alexander Home, to be the sign
and fruit of his triumph.

The recent developments in English poetry illustrate what
happens when, in a whole body of work, there is a failure to
preserve the necessary balance between two conceptions of art:
the conception of it as a means of knowing, and the conception
of it as a thing made.

It should not be necessary, at this distance from the *Biographia
Literaria*, to insist that art is not synonymous with craft. Yet one
of the most favoured ways of avoiding the general dilemma of
the modern artist is found in the view that the two words *are*
synonymous. Eric Gill's remark that 'the artist is not a special
kind of man; every man is a special kind of artist' is a sensible
comment on the nature of craft and of man's natural capacity
for it; but it says nothing at all about the nature of art. Even so,

it is very often used to deny that the artist as such has any special knowledge or vocation. And it is given philosophical respectability by being associated with the allegedly 'Thomist' slogan: 'Art is a judgment respecting a work to be made.'

Such a view is, however, easily disposed of. The key to the distinction between art and craft – a distinction which both these slogans tend to ignore – seems to me to lie in the idea of knowledge itself. It may be urged that the craftsman has a kind of knowledge; and so he has. But it is a knowledge concerned simply with the nature of his materials and with the techniques by which these materials can be made into an object, an artifact. If it were formulated in a series of statements – in a philosophy of craft – it would be seen to consist in knowledge *about* materials and their use. The artist, on the other hand, has a kind of knowledge which penetrates *into* things other than the nature and use of his materials, and which is, at the same time, both more immediate and more elevating. This knowledge becomes part of the process of composition itself, becomes the very material of the artist. It is incarnated, rather than built, in the work of art, while retaining its character as knowledge of reality. No transformation of this sort is possible, even if it were thought desirable, in the exercise of a craft.

But the craft view is held mainly by artistic reactionaries for whom the developments in the poetry of the last forty years are nothing but a wanton experiment with language. The reigning schools have over-balanced on the other side; their fall may be regarded as an instance of 'vaulting ambition which o'er-leaps itself'; but it would be more apt, I think, to regard it as the stumble of a thrower who has made a blind and desperate throw into the void. For them, art is knowledge, and nothing more; for some, it is direct knowledge of essences leading to prophetic speech; for others, it is the natural extension of the knowing self in an organic growth which he cannot of his own powers control. Some such view was necessary if poetry was to become a means of signifying 'faith in the absoluteness of the poetic image', a 'substitute spiritual institution'. The craft aspects of art, except for a number of rather obvious devices and shifts, tend to be ignored; for the kind of intellectual control denoted by 'craftsmanship' is seen as an artificial building-up of effects, in which purity of knowledge is clouded and its richness nullified.

I have dealt with certain of the general cultural reasons for the growth of this idea; and I have dealt with them by stressing their instability at the risk possibly of disguising their temporary value as a means of renewing language and perception. A treatment of the view itself on the level of a discussion in aesthetics would uncover in it a certain truth and a rather crippling falsehood. Nobody, not even the champions of 'organic poetry', really imagines that the great poems of the past just grew, as a plant grows, independent of control. Nor does anyone really imagine that the poet's control extended only to a little watering, and an occasional protection from frost.

As well as that, the metaphor of organic growth seems to me a singularly unhappy one in which to express the kind of life possessed by a poem. No language grows in a completely autonomous way, but rather through a series of attempts to adapt the human mind and senses to the necessities (internal as well as external) of actual, communal life. The same is true of any poem; it is possible only as the result of a life-time of controlled reactions to the same society which everyone inhabits; and in the art of composition, it can grow only by virtue of a similar control of experience. Max Harris once praised the English poet, Nicholas Moore, for his prolific output and ubiquitous presence; it seems he could write so many poems a week. This seems to me to give the game away; poetically, Nicholas Moore hardly exists, and he hardly ever did exist. One poem repeated ad infinitum is not a body of work. And it is paradoxical, to say the least, that the very people who stress the organic nature of any poem should be unwilling to ask that it be, in certain important respects, unique among its fellows. Uniqueness, however, is the result of craft working on each separate intuition; it is not to be found where art is regarded as knowledge of essences, because there both roots and gardener's hand are alike missing.

The truth is, that 'technique' has become an extra, a necessary accidental, a way of getting the final exciting gloss. In very few places is it regarded any longer as part of the very individuality of the artist engaged in the active grasp and moulding of his experience, as correlative with the artistic intuition itself. If we read Aristotle or Coleridge in the light of the artistic developments of the past two hundred years, we shall see that, for both of these great critics, that is precisely what technique is – a form of rational control which is neither arbitrary nor occasional, but which is demanded, naturally and ineluctably, by the subject-matter. And it is interesting to note that, despite their differing emphases, both writers thought poetry to present a unique kind of knowledge about the world as well as to be a unique kind of pleasure-giving form; it is quite instructive to note, further, that they saw poetry as possessed of a deep and indispensable function in serving the moral and social needs of man, simply by being what its own aesthetic rules make it.

Such a view is possible only when certain conditions are fulfilled, certain standards observed, in the reader's expectations concerning art in general. In the first place, an adequate balance must be preserved between the idea of poetry as a means of knowledge and the idea of it as a thing consciously made – indeed, these two elements must be seen as requiring each other almost as cause requires its appropriate effect. There must be, too, a sense of the limitations of poetry, and hence an assigning it its due place in the hierarchy of cultural activities. This, of course, argues a certain agreement about basic beliefs. There ought, finally, to be less neurotic insistence on poetry as 'communication', and a calm acceptance of it as a source of communion between men, based on its presentation of the human mystery in fully human terms. Neither the good reader nor the good poet is simply passive in the face of a poem; they both take an eager interest in it, an interest which may perhaps be characterized by the term 'active self-surrender'. It is obvious, furthermore, that a stress on 'communication' will become most imperative at that point of a culture's development where the vision to be communicated comes to be seen as a completely personal one which justifies itself and so supplants other, and more traditional truths.

None of these necessary standards is generally present in any culture today; and he would be a humourless man who claimed that they were the standards by which he was consistently guided in his response to poetry. They are not present, either, in Australia or Australians. I do not wish to exaggerate the importance of our poetic achievement, which is limited both in breadth and depth. We have a temporary advantage, not in the possession of positive critical and creative standards, but in the absence of those contrary forces (I cannot call them standards) which many of the European poets have set up as alternatives to them.

In the foregoing pages, I have put my feeling about the trends in modern poetry in several different and complementary forms, which may seem, from the very compression of the analysis, as several distinct charges. They are not intended as charges at all. I have no wish to align myself with such a critic as D. S. Savage when, happily working the bolt of his critical rifle, he lines up all available modern writers in his sights. No one should be more sensible than I of the imaginative life which has attended the various movements in poetry over the past forty years. For all their terror and incompleteness, such poets as Yeats and Rilke were full of a burning wisdom, which effectively sets limits to man's achievement at the same time as it increases his desire for it; certainly no Australian poet can compare with them. But the long and involved apologies for art with which the post-Renaissance world has increasingly comforted itself have now found their own hell – the hell of social rejection and of their own inconsequence. Much poetry, as well as criticism, has become an attempt to defend and justify nothing else than itself; and the very attempt, in its despair and pride, leads to a kind of spiritual nausea.

One would be foolish to expect every poet to conform to one's image of a 'complete poet', even if one were foolish enough to entertain such an image in the first place. Yet we too are under the necessity of writing, and for us it is a necessity of the present, having in it something of urgency. The process of poetry did not end, just as it did not begin, with Eliot or Thomas; it is a process which continues through a number of people now writing (a few of them very convincingly indeed), and which has become somewhat harder to continue because of the partial success of the 'raids on the inarticulate' made by Eliot and Thomas. Therefore, it ought not to be conceived as wanton and destructive criticism if I state that the imaginative climate of the moment is in certain respects limited and unhealthy, and if I choose to dwell on these elements rather than on the richness of association which, through a confused struggle, poetry has lately regained. There is no question of personalities, or of an *argumentum ad hominem*. Most of the people I have mentioned have 'done the state some service'; two or three of them have done it a distinct honour. Yet taken as a whole, far from solving the mystery of man who, faced with the extraordinary breakdown of his security, sets himself the task of creating his own world in the light of God, they have not even posed that mystery with a sufficient cogency.

Kenneth Slessor: Realist or Romantic?

THERE SEEMS to be a vague and generally-held notion that Kenneth Slessor is a major Australian poet. No serious attempt, however, has as yet been made to arrive at a careful critical assessment of his work: the assumption hovers in the air undefended and unchallenged.

There is, at any rate, plenty of material on which to work. Slessor has published four books of poetry at various times within the third and fourth decades of this century; most of them are not easy to come by, and the poet himself has chosen in any case to make from these volumes a selection of what he considers his most significant poems. The collection is his volume *One Hundred Poems*. The critic may follow him in regarding these as an adequate field for his enquiry. And, looking briefly at them, we may see massively demonstrated the extent to which Slessor was a pioneer in modern Australian poetry; a slightly more extensive glance will force us to ask, with growing confusion, in what field and in what direction was his pioneering done.

A possible reason for the ambiguity of his position strikes us when we look at his early works, those composed (as we are told in the index to *One Hundred Poems*) between 1919 and 1926. In subject-matter, conception, and technique, he is to a large extent outside the tradition of Australian poetry – and even of the English poetry of this century. The titles give us an indication – 'Pan at Lane Cove', 'Marco Polo', 'Heine in Paris', 'Thieves' Kitchen'; and the treatment is generally in keeping with the hint of romantic grotesquerie given in the titles. His friends probably have had something to do with all this; and, indeed, much of Slessor's early poetry, in its attempt to bring together words and the world, seems to be a marriage by proxy, with Hugh McCrae obligingly standing-in for the aspiring young poet, and Norman Lindsay mock-heroically officiating. 'Thieves' Kitchen' is a very good example:

> Good roaring pistol-boys, brave lads of gold,
> Good roistering easy maids, blown cock-a-hoop
> On floods of tavern-steam, I greet you! Drunk
> With wild Canary, drowned in wines of old,
> I'll swear your round, red faces dive and swim
> Like clouds of fire-fish in a waxen tide,
> And these are seas of smoke we thieves behold.

The nature of the approach is obvious. No attempt is made by the poet to individualize the 'good roaring pistol-boys', as even Villon did, or to indicate their role in the human situation. The conception is a cliché, and so are the various items in the picture; while the language is a sort of forced eloquence, and the subject is treated through a violent and confused accumulation of images. The only thing of value that remains with the reader is an impression of sheer zest in the picture-making, and of the desperate inconsequence of the performance.

These early poems are in a very real sense Romantic – showing the strong attraction felt by their author towards the grotesque and exaggerated elements of experience, and towards a raffish sensuousness. (Here, for the exponent of Coleridge's aesthetic seeking to explain his master, here is a fitting example of a poetry which is the product of random imagings and of a surface will.) These qualities stand behind the typically Romantic attitude to expression which has just been mentioned. It is not unusual to find such qualities and attitudes in the work of a young poet. But in Slessor's case it would be foolish to assume (as most people do) that they give way in the later poetry to a direct realism. It is true that the poetic world of the later poems is the harder and more immediate, and that a greater part of it is filled with the items of everyday experience. Yet all too often we find, even in the very last poems, the same imagery, the same forced eloquence of language, the same emphasis on a dream (or is it nightmare?) condition of life which so disturb us in the early work:

> Uncles who burst on childhood, from the East,
> Blown from air, like bearded ghosts arriving,
> And are, indeed, a kind of guessed-at ghost
> Through mumbled names at dinner-tables moving,

Bearers of parrots, bonfires of blazing stones,
Their pockets fat with riches out of reason,
Meerschaum and sharks'-teeth, ropes of China coins,
And weeds and seeds and berries blowzed with poison —

This, fittingly enough, is titled 'To the Poetry of Hugh McCrae'.
The big advance that Slessor has made in the years which separate this from his earliest work is that here he accomplishes a
sort of finality to his poetic thought of which he was seemingly
incapable twenty years before; and, even more important than
this, he is actively seeking such a finality in his poetry. The
poem in question ends:

(Look in this harsher glass, and I will show you
The daylight after the darkness, and the morning
After the midnight, and after the night the day
After the year after, terribly returning.)

We live by these, your masks and images,
We breathe in this, your quick and borrowed body;
But you take passage on the ruffian seas,
And you are vanished in the dark already.

Nevertheless, this poem has qualities which one might have supposed more typical of Slessor's early work; and the point should
be clear that the tinge of Romantic grotesquerie is not simply a
foible of his early days, but is rather a recurring and directing
element in his poetry. If in the later work it is less unmixed
with the elements of everyday experience, it is nevertheless used
there with the air of an exile yearning for his true home. All
through the poetry dated from 1927 to 1939, we are liable to
come upon poems which are models of exact and whimsical
observation. There are, of course, occasional illustrations from
the first volume, for example, the

Gas flaring on the yellow platform; voices running up
   and down;
Milk-tins in cold dented silver; half awake I stare,
Pull up the blind, blink out — all sounds are drugged;

of 'The Night Ride'; but they are rare. From the middle section,
'Wild Grapes', 'Waters', 'Crow Country', 'Metempsychosis', immediately come to mind; and, of course, that most sprightly of

his short poems, 'Country Towns', which seems to have brought
itself to the attention of most Australian anthologists as Slessor's
anthology-piece:

> At the School of Arts, a broadsheet lies
> Sprayed with the sarcasm of flies:
> 'The Great Golightly Family
> Of Entertainers Here To-night' –
> Dated a year and a half ago,
> But left there, less from carelessness
> Than from a wish to seem polite.

This is not so much wit as a flash of keen observation from
a man who has put himself into immediate and direct sympathy
with his subject. The last two lines exactly express the diffidence
of many country people in dealing with the affairs of their
strolling players. Yet the distinction between wit and observation
is a significant one. For a man with a feeling for the grotesque
and an obviously sardonic temperament, there is surprisingly
little wit in Slessor, and almost no humour at all. He is as unlike
A. D. Hope in this as in his attitude to poetic form.

The added hardness of line and imagery is certainly welcome,
for it means that Slessor has begun to locate the perennial
problems of man in the ordinary affairs of the men of his own
time, and that he is now less inclined to try to escape in his
poetry a consideration of those problems. He has, moreover,
begun to approach a poetic solution to them through the world
of sense data which is the first and best repository of the artist's
wisdom. Yet he is obviously striving throughout his poetic
development for a realism which will not require him to abandon
his bravura effects or to stifle his Romantic zest. And the result,
even in the best of his minor poems, is something which is more
properly called 'physicalism' than 'realism'–a preoccupation
with grasping, in one desperate swoop, all the variety, all the
hard physicality of sense-experience, till so much detail is
brought into the poem that not only meaning but the distinctive
lines of material things themselves are made blurred and indecisive. A good example of this is the much-quoted 'Last Trams'
(ii):

> Then, from the skeletons of trams,
> Gazing at lighted rooms, you'll find
> The black and Röntgen diagrams
> Of window-plants across the blind

That print their knuckleduster sticks,
Their buds of gum, against the light
Like negatives of candlesticks
Whose wicks are lit by fluorite.

This is no doubt an acute conception; but, despite the hardness of outline, it is too much clogged, baffled by its detail. The irony is that, when so much has been given up for the thrust and spontaneous flow of images, that thrust itself tends to be deflected, that flow to become dissipated and to fade in the fine sand of words. There is, in consequence, a vague yet disturbing air of frenzy about almost all Slessor's poems – the poems of joy as well as those of sorrow. One can detect a desperation in the act of writing itself, as though each poem is an activity divorced from any spiritual serenity, an attempt to get as much as possible into the poet's picture before the whole world disappears.

It would be generally true to say that the basis of Slessor's art is rhetorical. This point, because of the difficulty of clarification, deserves an essay to itself, and it cannot be adequately treated here. Yet I may be permitted to approach it obliquely, while seeming to talk of something else. His best poems are nearly all concerned with simple situations or with people. He has a truly imposing Dramatis Personae, of whom the most frequent performer is himself, considered always ironically, mock-heroically, or with a sort of fierce disdain; for the rest, his characters are drawn from among his friends, from history and the novel, from fellow artists, and, most important of all, men of the sea.

The treatment is always dramatic in the extreme, and the language is almost always rhetorical; the words and images are not used, as they are in Browning or the early Eliot, to fix a character in his individual fullness in his particular milieu, but rather to give the surroundings, to provide an occasion for Slessor to talk about life, or to establish a note of adventure in whatever situation has been vaguely delineated. The person concerned, one feels, is not intended to occupy the centre of the stage, but to stand in the wings while, with repeated reference to his presence, the author strews his belongings behind the footlights. So we are less interested in Captain Dobbin than in

Captain Dobbin's room, packed with the junk of past adventures;
and less concerned with the exciting relics themselves than with
the sea, of whose conquest they are the trophies. The graceful
and moving last stanza establishes the destiny not so much of
Captain Dobbin as of the sea from which he is almost a by-
product, another relic:

> Flowers rocked far down
> And white, dead bodies that were anchored there
> In marshes of spent light.
> Blue Funnel, Red Funnel,
> The ships went over them, and bells in engine-rooms
> Cried to their bowels of flaring oil,
> And stokers groaned and sweated with burnt skins,
> Clawed to their shovels.
> But quietly in his room,
> In his little cemetery of sweet essences
> With fond memorial-stones and lines of grace,
> Captain Dobbin went on reading about the sea.

At its best and most sincere, this approach is extremely effective. 'Five Visions of Captain Cook', which should be known to
every Australian, enables Slessor to approach Cook's voyage
from five different points of view, with accompanying changes
in treatment and technique. The result is a memorable though
uneven poem, with his ever-present eloquence directed by a
controlling idea, and kept for the most part in subjection to
definite and contrasting sentiments. (The pounding metre and
generalized language of the first part, for example, contrast
effectively with the whimsical tenderness and gently varying
rhythms of the third). It is worth noting, however, that this is
one of the few poems in which a real character portrayal is
attempted, and a real assessment of values.

With these things in mind, it is with a shock of delighted
surprise that one comes upon such a poem as 'Sleep', in which
there is not only one controlling idea, but also one controlling
image, with reference to which all other images are deployed.
This initial control of structure allows Slessor to concentrate
on rhythm and diction – allows him, as he so seldom allows himself, to be a complete and satisfying craftsman.[1] Thus we get a

---

[1] I am fully aware that this statement will be regarded either as insolent
incomprehension or as boyish paradox; for Slessor is often spoken of as the

lyric which has the depth of wholly convincing statement, and
which is completely rounded by the artist's mind.

> Then I shall bear you down my estuary,
> Carry you and ferry you to burial mysteriously,
> Take you and receive you,
> Consume you, engulf you,
> In the huge cave, my belly, lave you
> With huger waves continually.

Even in this small poem, we have evidence of Slessor's main
preoccupations. A study of his recurring themes and images
will show that he is probably the most 'preoccupied' poet writing
in Australia today. It seems that there are themes from which
he can never escape, no matter what may be the alleged subject
of any of his poems; and which are insisted on so frequently
and so forcefully that (if we may use a phrase which has become
peculiarly a part of the American language) they attain the
status of myths. Time (written often with a capital), the sea, the
sea-faring adventurer – these are the Slessor myths; and it is
when they are combined that they are used most clearly and
most effectively, as in 'Five Visions of Captain Cook', for instance,
and in 'Five Bells'. Yet there is something underlying even
these basic motifs and giving them coherence. In almost all his
poems, Slessor seems ultimately concerned with the fact of flux.
Time for him is not only the enemy of human plans, and so an
active force; it is also an element, into which things and people
move, within which they are momentarily poised, and from
which they are irresistibly borne. If a symbol is needed for this
eternally destructive movement of time, then the sea will serve
very well; and the significance of the sailor in Slessor's poetic
world is that of man himself, adventuring forth upon the flux to
which he will eventually be reduced.

When this is considered, perhaps it is inevitable that Slessor's
view of the human situation should be a sensational one, and
that it should involve so many examples of the exaggerated and

---

finest craftsman among the modern Australian poets. And if craftsman be
taken to mean 'technical virtuoso', I agree. He is a splendid virtuoso. But
craftsmanship differs from virtuosity in this: that it concerns not only the
ability to use materials, but the ability to choose the right materials in the
right context. And Slessor did not mature enough in his grasp of his materials
to do this consistently.

the grotesque. In such a view of life as this, Caesar's only role is to symbolize the preoccupation of a modern poet; and one's speculations will turn very often on what it would be like to have been someone else. We have Slessor's 'Metempsychosis' for example:

> Suddenly to become John Benbow, walking down William Street
> With a tin trunk and a five-pound note, looking for a place to eat,
> And a peajacket the colour of a shark's behind
> That a Jew might buy in the morning . . .

This is not an unusual view of life in modern poetry; it is an important part of the whole neo-Romantic conception. It is rare, however, to find it insisted on so completely and with such intensity of focus as it is in Slessor; and he certainly does not ignore the necessity of providing himself with certain symbols of permanence, which can also be used as vantage-points from which to get a perspective on the flux of human experience. I take it the Harbour is one of these. Sydney Harbour appears so frequently in his poetry that it is an essential part of his land-scape. Its role is stated almost explicitly in 'Winter Dawn' and 'Captain Dobbin', as well as in 'Five Bells'. It is not only a point of refuge, it is also a point of view.

'Five Bells' is the poem which he has chosen to occupy pride of last place in *One Hundred Poems,* and it is certainly his finest poem. It is, in fact, probably the last of the poems in chrono-logical order; but it is also in a very real sense a *summing-up* of the themes and dominant images which recur so much in his earlier poetry. I do not suggest that it is intended to act as a summing-up, but merely that it does, almost as a matter of course. And it does so very finely; it may not be claiming too much to say that 'Five Bells' is one of the two or three best poems written in Australia.

It is here that we find all his main individual themes brought together, but brought together at such a pitch of intensity that they are lifted beyond the status of preoccupation into a sort of vision — a vision which is admittedly tortured and obscure, a vision of dissolution rather than of resurrection, but a vision nevertheless. Perhaps this can be explained by the fact that all these themes have been given a powerful focus, an intimate personal concern, in Slessor's grief for his 'long dead friend'.

His image for death is drowning, the sea is the agent not only of death but of dissolution, and Time is used for the first time as a ship's bell which, at the same time as it rings Joe's knell, recalls him to Slessor's mind. Once again the Harbour is Slessor's point of reference, the vantage-point from which he can give coherence to his agonized meditation. It is, indeed, a perfect focus for his musings, for it has him within sight of the materials for them:

> Where have you gone? The tide is over you,
> The turn of midnight water's over you,
> As time is over you, and mystery,
> And memory, the flood that does not flow.
> You have no suburb, like those easier dead
> In private berths of dissolution laid —
> The tide goes over, the waves ride over you
> And let their shadows down like shining hair,
> But they are Water; and the sea-pinks bend
> Like lilies in your teeth, but they are Weed;
> And you are only part of an Idea.

It is a powerful, a nervous, a surprisingly varied poem. It proceeds from a tense, concentrated opening, in which the sound of a ship's bell ringing the night hours brings back to the poet the memory of his friend; through certain dramatic glimpses of Joe's life, separated by Slessor's own anguished longings; to the almost wearily expansive close, an acquiescence bred of exhaustion. In the process, a concern for one man's death becomes imperceptibly concern for all mankind. It is not only an expression of grief, but also a protest against death, and a questioning of life itself. The great variety of rhythm, the great suggestion of oppression in the flood of memory that will not flow, prevent us calling it an exercise in self-pity — or, indeed, in locating any such melting sentiment in it at all. Yet it is obviously of himself that the poet is thinking. Because of this fact, not despite it, Joe's death is the death, actual or impending, of every man.

And it is significant that such a cosmic anguish results in Slessor's best writing about the sea. It is in 'Five Bells' that his obsession with flux and his faculty of close observation are most successfully brought together, for the theme is such, his realization of it such, that there need be no dichotomy between them.

The fluxive action of the sea gives free play, under his personal and cosmic grief, to his sensuality of imagery, his 'highly developed tactile sense. I do not want to suggest that it is merely a seascape with emotional overtones; it has, in fact, considerable variety of scene. The drab rooms in Melbourne and Sydney (those oddly dated rooms), the bush walks, the desolate headlands, and the landlubber's graveyard, all help to give the poem its undoubted poignancy; yet each of these scenes is somehow fused with an awareness of the 'watery bier', each is somehow drenched and dampened by the arrogant sea-spray. It is a poem which, at every stage of its development, remains acutely conscious of its central theme and symbol.

It is also, as I have said, a summing-up of his main themes in other poems; indeed, it repeats several of the key phrases from his earlier poems. This, I feel, is not a mere coincidence. 'Five Bells' is, in a sense, Slessor's manifesto, the occasion for a recapitulation of all he has to say in poetry, and of all the ways he has discovered of imaging that statement successfully.

It is this which makes us wonder whether he will ever write again. For what is there to say that has not already been said? What poetic opportunity can now be given to Slessor greater than the opportunity he has so powerfully seized in 'Five Bells'? Well, there was one thing more to say – one further stage to carry his feeling of helpless compassion and of self-mistrust; and he carried his feelings that one step in 'Beach Burial':

> And each cross, the driven stake of tidewood,
> Bears the last signature of men,
> Written with such perplexity, with such bewildered pity,
> The words choke as they begin –

But there can be no further step along this path; in this poem already, compassion has become self-sickened, ill with its own force; and compassion – helpless compassion – is the only thing Slessor seems to have left. It is a noble, an inspiring thing; no other Australian poet has it in such measure, or even in such a kind; but if the poet is to develop in it, the compassion itself will have to be capable of developing in quality. And this he seems unable to ensure. He has no further occasion for writing.

A man's past life makes his present opportunity, or at least accounts for its depth and dimension. And, so far as I know,

Slessor has not written since the war. At that time, he seems to have published two pieces; and of those the only one which is notable is the poignant, beautifully-balanced short poem to which I have already alluded. It was the war which collaborated with his personal life to exact this one poem from him; it is significant that the war could produce from him only the one. To put it in another way, Slessor no longer 'has anything to say'. And this, although it alarm and disappoint us, ought not really to surprise us. Despite the chatter of the critics, he is not really an 'intellectual' poet. It is true that he has always eschewed the easy path of Georgian nature description, and has gone his own way. But his poetry shows that he was led on that way not by the demands of his intellect continually to discover and re-create the deepest truths of the human situation, but by the Romantic desperation of his preoccupations. For all his occasional joy, there runs throughout his poetry a faint ground-bass of disgust with life. In 'Five Bells', this has been brought forward as an open protest against life. No poet of Slessor's kind can do more than this – make his preoccupations public. This is what *he* has done; but it is not what we expect of an 'intellectual' poet.

The Development of R. D. FitzGerald

TO HAVE greatness thrust upon you may be an experience pleasant or unpleasant, according to your opinion of yourself. R. D. FitzGerald has had thrust on him the mantle of Great Australian Poet; and I suspect that he finds it unpleasant. The title, in any case, is a silly and ambiguous one. What ought to be said of him is that he is always an interesting poet, always an honest one, always a courageous one; and that he is sometimes a good one. To say this is to say quite a good deal; it must surely be less galling to the poet himself than the claims which have sometimes been made on his behalf.

When we approach the whole of his poetry, we find a body of work which, for sheer weight of output combined with apparent variation in manner and technique, would probably find no parallel in modern Australian poetry. The bulk is impressive; and a surprisingly large portion of it is interesting. The variation is both illuminating and encouraging; for it is by no means an arbitrary change from one style to a second and thence to a third, but a steady growth in the apprehension of formal problems – a growth which has produced its own technical resources or, shall we say, formal answers.

And such bulk, such variation, conceal a great persistence of theme. All FitzGerald's poetry seems to me to be about the one thing, no matter how tentative its manifestations or how disguised its sources. That one thing is time – more especially, time in its backwardness, time past yet flowing forward, time as the individual inherits it. One may say that he has devoted all his life to exploring this mystery – not, mind you, to solving a problem, but to exploring a mystery, which comes from his hand as intact as when it entered. The only problems with which he concerns himself are technical ones; the theme to which those technical shifts are applied as means, retains its full mysterious force.

FitzGerald is, and always has been, a poet of romantic sentiment. It is a little beside the point to shove him categorically into the latter-day school of Donne. He conceives human experi-

ence in that mobile impressionistic way which we label Romantic
in order to oppose it to Classic solidity and calm. And his
attitudes, one might almost say his poses, have always been those
of the man who 'accepts' a little too indiscriminately, who is
too much at home with the flux which, so many men persuade
themselves, is the basic fact of the human situation. His very
early work is crude in form, and sentimental in statement. From
there he has proceeded, by a series of creative manoeuvres, into
a greater range of ideas and a greater maturity in his grasp of
the central fascinating issue. Yet his poetry has, at the same
time, become more adventurous in form. These blessings are
mixed ones. For it has also become craggier and rougher in outline, further removed in texture and movement alike from what
the practice of the post-Romantic period has disposed us to
welcome in poetry.

For these very reasons, it is virtually impossible to treat his
work otherwise than in chronological sequence. Such a method,
when announced by an essayist, may well seem a recipe for
tedium; but in FitzGerald's case it is unavoidable.

Is he a poet of the twenties? Yes, in his beginnings, in his
early, crude, ambivalent Romanticism. Is he a poet of the
thirties? Yes; for this was the period of his formation as a poet,
of his best-known utterances, of his first attempt to write a
majestic long poem, of his entry into the hard development of
modern Australian poetry. Is he a poet of the forties? His most
individual poems were written in that decade; it was then that
he began to teach us how certain technical problems, certain
modes of address, certain dramatic emphases, could be part of
the growth of our poetry.

His first book, *To Meet the Sun*, was published when he was
twenty-seven; and it is a surprisingly immature book for a man
of such an age to have produced. These poems are, without
exception, juvenilia – and poetically uninteresting juvenilia at
that. Conventional in attitude, barnacled with archaic words
and poses, they offer us, if we take them as a whole, nothing
more interesting than a very young man's manifesto against
dullness and conformity. Yet there are hints, peeps of a positive
theme which is later to emerge and claim his talent. Beside the
vague sense that any aspiration is worth while so long as it has

been freed from hypocrisy and meanness, there is something else : the sense of human continuity :

> I think in your forgotten tombs
> you feel through me to-day's warm bliss,
> because you once saw other blooms
> in springtimes far removed from this.

Here, crude and off-pitch, is the note which we are to find very often in his later poetry, the idea that the dead may experience present pleasure by having shared it in their life-time. Should we take it all very seriously? I should say yes; for it is not only a young man's fancy turned to thoughts of death, but a repetition of an insight which is often again to be repeated. It is by no means a 'mystical' idea. On the contrary, it reveals an emphasis on present experience as the only one which has any meaning. It is not precisely the traditional cry of *carpe diem*, but an idea which can be more exactly located in a philosophy – that of materialist vitalism, the silliest and most romantic of all creeds.

In the ninth poem in the 'Moonlight Acre' series, this thought becomes :

> So when I clasp you here I keep
> all that dead lovers have desired,
> waken their bodies from long sleep
> and their dreams, changeless and untired.

> Held thus, you become drawn breath of any
> who have been loved – once named, once known;
> and the brief lives of that white many
> you hand on, deathless and your own.

> There is only this embrace at last
> anywhere; others touched you once,
> but I touch all the present and past
> and the wide sky's uncounted suns.

But this is a love poem; and the poet as lover has licence to say almost anything he pleases. Such an insight, in a love poem, may attain (as it does here) a balance and vibrancy which remove it from the level of conscious attitude. This is a good poem, and it offers us a lovely comment on the nature of love. Life, however, stubbornly retaining its initial capital, is another matter, and ought not to be treated so lightly. What is natural and affecting in a love poem may well appear *jejune* in a more philosophical work.

And we may go on through this second volume, playing variations on themes which were established years before: seeing FitzGerald work out certain implications of the opposition between life and the creative imagination – the moonlight of the imagination being pierced (but not fertilized?) by the pine's dark steeple of sense reality; the soul in turn struggling from the 'somnambulist life-in-a-mist' of that life into the greater reality of the mind which can range time past and time future; and we realize with FitzGerald that life is a ceaseless dialectic of opposing forces.

Not, perhaps, a very impressive swag of ideas. But they are not offered to us as ideas. Abstracted from their fleshy context, they seem solemn, conventional and circumscribed. Fleshed and arrayed for the street, they are strong, courageous, possessed of a hard joy. Even at this stage of his development, the poet is being more factual, more incarnational, than his master Norman Lindsay. He is already nursing the germ of his later dramatic works.

The reason, I suppose, is that the poems in the 'Moonlight Acre' and 'Copernicus' series are no longer 'personal' lyrics in the sense in which *To Meet the Sun* was personal. FitzGerald is still relying on a lyric tone and using lyric forms, as he continues to do up to 'The Hidden Bole'. But the conception of these lyrics is of an implicitly dramatic kind. All of them are based, of course, on personal experience; but whereas some (nos. vii, x, and xvii in the 'Moonlight Acre' series, for example) express a personal emotion arising out of a directly personal situation, most of them are lyrics which are also concerned with making general statements about life. They are not, for the most part, generalized in diction and imagery; for the general statements are symbolized or given a dramatic form. But they are not simply songs, either.

There are certain dangers in this approach, and FitzGerald, in his encounters with them, has not always been successful. Very many of the lyrics fail as wholes, even though they have successful, and sometimes lovely, parts: and their failure stems precisely from the fact that each poem is made to develop in the way a lyric poem develops, but the thought is too involved, the imagery too various, to be easily carried by such a simple and spontaneous form. He is trying to say too much, and is relying on too many disconnected images with which to say it. Such a method tends to destroy, by a sort of inner mining or burrowing, the lyrical force which, taken as a surface effect, is often charming and graceful:

> Boring the darkness, these eyes burn
> into reality, return
> from the somnambulist
> life-in-a-mist
>
> of long imprisonment behind
> masonry caging-in the mind —
> impervious and dense
> ashlar of sense —
>
> wherein there is only matter such
> as the sight tells of and the touch:
> dream-woven filmy veil,
> flowerlike and frail.

At first sight, this seems a lovely and satisfying form, because the most obvious fact about it is the lyric movement and grace. On a second look, the movement stumbles, the grace narrows and wrinkles; for we realize that FitzGerald is trying to say not one thing, but a number of things, about the relationship of the 'real' world of the imagination with that other world whose values are expressed by the tyranny of the senses. It is not impossible, though it is certainly difficult, for the lyric poet to make statements of this kind while preserving the lyric purity of his verse. But in FitzGerald's case, the task is made even more difficult by the fact that he seems incapable of thinking except in images. In three tiny verses, we have at least five images to indicate one thing. 'The darkness', 'somnambulist life-in-a-mist', 'masonry caging-in the mind', 'ashlar of sense', and 'dream-woven filmy veil', all refer (or seem to refer) to the tyranny of the senses. And when they are brought together in such a short space, they must appear a most incongruous collection of generalized images. The very syntax is

disturbed by the over-crowding, and becomes an additional
agent of confusion.

The same fault (though often without a disturbed syntax) is
found, in varying degress, in most of these lyrics. The poems
which are least affected are, I think, those sustained by a strong
core of direct personal feeling, and those in which FitzGerald's
dramatic sense is found emerging to draw the images together.
One or two of the personal lyrics, influenced as they are by the
practice of Christopher Brennan, have some startlingly lovely
touches; and these poems are generally both congruous in
imagery and constant in lyrical tone. The more 'dramatic'
lyrics are sometimes equally successful; for in them lyrical
feeling is projected on to some situation external to the poet,
and a situation which is susceptible to forthright utterance:

> Fought for the new toys barely made:
> sea and cool air and souls of men –
> whence this unquiet that again
> raids and is met with counter-raid;
> while you, lone traveller, undelayed,
> click shoe to pebble on that fringe
> where sky and earth impinge.
>
> Go your way: why should you look or heed
> who inherit also the strife? What breath
> drawn by men but is aimed at death? –
> arrows unequal to the need.
> In your own contest, this, good speed!
> Behind you the hooves charge: skulls break:
> old cries shudder and wake.

This is Brennan made extravert, his Irish melancholy hardened
by an Australian swagger. FitzGerald's symbol is more open,
more obvious, more accessible, than most of Brennan's; it can
be more easily manoeuvred and made into a dramatic device.

How far the lyrics in 'Moonlight Acre', or in 'Copernicus',
form a genuine sequence, is open to question. It may be that in
each case there is some development of a theme; but not a
readily perceptible one. What seems to unify the poems in each
series is a certain repetition of image, a certain consistency of
poetic attitude and texture. And I, for one, feel some greater
unity to be desirable. I am not agitating for a cut-and-dried
pattern among the poems – what the alarming American critics

call a *schema* (or is it *schemata*?); I am simply remarking that it
would be pleasant to have such a unity in these poems that they
help to illumine, even to explain, one another. And they are,
after all, relatively obscure. FitzGerald is making certain that his
important images have a symbolic effect, but it is difficult in each
case to know what the symbol stands for, and FitzGerald does
not seem interested in telling us explicitly enough to make the
effort of investigation worth while. With three or four excep-
tions, these pieces may be called an impressionistic poetry which
attempts, without being very explicit, to achieve a symbolic
effect by the very recurrence and arrangement of the images.
Such an approach, in lyrical verse, cannot help being rather a
distraction. The immature use of poetic phrasing on which I
have commented is found, to an extreme degree, in 'Essay on
Memory'. This has always seemed to me a stodgy and boring
poem. It is public utterance, verse with a mission; the muse is
here making one of her rare stage-appearances; and as she seems
too unbuttoned and a little tipsy, she is not quite equal to the
occasion. Nothing sustains her in her plight – neither the chair-
manship of strong intellectual control, nor the strong arm of a
directed emotion:

> This hour, a gulp in the long throat of the past,
> swallows what once was future, but soon spent;
> this hour is a touch of hands, an accident
> of instants meeting in unechoing vast:
> it is a rail that bursts before the flourish
> of black manes and time's haste; it fails our need –
> now must decision be brief, must jump or perish
> under the feet and fury of stampede.

The lines are too packed and tense not only for easy assimilation, but for assimilation as poetry at all. The thought is not a
difficult nor an involved one; but by the time we have read the
first four lines of the over-insistent eight, we have given up trying
to remember their meaning. As I have remarked, FitzGerald
seems incapable of thinking except in images; yet here, as in
other places, he does not give his images room to breathe. If I
may follow his example in abruptly varying the metaphor, the
images are packed so tightly together that the reverberations of
each are muffled by the nearness of the others. As he gained in

experience between 'Copernicus' and 'Essay on Memory', his tendency to over-write has not lessened, but has actually increased.

It would be easy to give a false impression. This is not a poetry of particularly involved statement; it is not, in the usual sense, even obscure. The fault is one of balance in the writing. FitzGerald is really attempting to say something definite and clear, but his natural talent too often defeats him in the saying. The thing he is saying is in most cases so general that he apparently feels it can be stated only through images, through the creation of an individual world of imagery in which the idea may be presented to the reader in all its immediacy. To use his own phrase, he is 'making ideas concrete'; but in 'Essay on Memory', at least, he is doing it in such a way as to make the process of re-translation difficult. He is attempting, I think, to do something similar to what Hopkins achieved so magnificently at times in his use of inscape – to give a statement about the meaning of things and at the same time to give the *feel* of the things themselves.

Whatever the nature of the attempt, it succeeds in the best poems of the two lyric sequences, and it fails in 'Essay on Memory'. Possibly, in the later poem, FitzGerald found himself oppressed by the effort of adjustment to a new literary form and emphasis. By the time of 'The Hidden Bole', which immediately precedes 'Essay on Memory' in his development, he has abandoned the purely lyric scope, and embarks on a series of longer poems, which are to engage most of his creative attention for seventeen years. He has abandoned the scope of the lyric, but not its style and emphasis. That abandonment is not to be made until 'Essay on Memory'.

Both poems may be regarded as poems of transition between his lyrical work and the later dramatic work; and so they partake of both elements. 'The Hidden Bole' is the more lyrical – and is, in fact, a sort of extended philosophical lyric. 'Essay on Memory' is the more 'dramatic' work, and is an uneasy structure indeed; yet it does show the tortured and rather desperate echoes of FitzGerald the lyricist. If previously the Irishman had assumed an Australian swagger, now he is turned German and plunges along with an arthritic goose-step.

These poems provide material for mutual comparison. For in neither of them is the dramatist's interest in human nature made the principal source of balance. In each, there is one sustaining image, which is intended to have the force of a symbol, and to dominate all its auxiliary images. In 'The Hidden Bole', it is the image of Pavlova dancing, the symbol of a beauty timeless yet transient. In 'Essay on Memory', it is the rain, symbol at once of obliteration and the creative memory.

It is unnecessary to give any account of the manner in which these thoughts are worked out in their respective poems. Certainly, the brief mention which I have made of their themes is sufficient to show that each poem has a dialectical structure, and is a pattern of question, objection, and answer; in each the value of the central symbol is ambiguous, because it raises as many questions as it purports to settle. And this fact alone makes them both interesting; for FitzGerald unflinchingly faces the questions as *they* confront *him;* the poetry is not an excuse for facing in the opposite direction from the one in which the poet affects to be facing. Yet, despite its unnecessary length, 'The Hidden Bole' presents a much more clear-cut pattern of question and response. Paradoxically, the simple lyrical attitudes help it here. It sings both question and response; it does not, as the later poem does, rant both statements till they become indistinguishable in the one blur of shouting.

It comes at the stage when FitzGerald's lyrical impulse was still strong and dominant, but when it had a sufficiently urgent question on which to play. The stanza-form is a difficult yet challenging one for a thoughtful poet; and in his best sections, he has used it to produce what we may call a 'dance of language' — that balance of consonant and vowel, of inflection and broader phrase which gives such a forceful grace to Yeats' poetry of the middle period, to 'A Prayer for My Daughter', for example. In FitzGerald, the dance is lighter, more tinkling, has less body and inevitability:

> Death lets her dance on always through my mind —
> is there a grave could close away Giselle
> when music calls her, when lorn flutes impel,
> and necromancing strings that cry and quiver?
> No curtain falls. Eyes, were you drunk or blind

not knowing her steps although you watched their thief,
the wind's toe-pointing leaf,
not seeing her swiftness chase the pebbled river?
She is the prisoned sunshine that became
delicate contour of escaping fire;
she is the snowflake blown upon the flame –
song and the melting wraith of song's desire.

Only one age could reach her, being stacked
on the thick labour of piled other ages:
only one page among time's handwrit pages
could find right context, turn of phrase, wise word,
to form her sentence, rhyme her into fact.
So does she crown our thought, all thought involve –
as all sweet tones resolve
into the twilight chiming of a bird.
Fade twilight; bird give over: the immense
murmur of night halts at your edge of air –
I praise your triumph for its transience,
that the notes pass and fair dies into fair.

'I praise'; praising is a good thing to be doing when faced with
a philosophical problem. Some readers may find elements in
his diction excessively sweet, excessively romantic. Yet the
poem as a whole is a forceful bestowal of form on romantic
passion; and the tendency to gush is arrested by the very formal
strictness, which gives FitzGerald so much freedom of development.

In the interval between this poem and 'Essay on Memory', he
lost one poetic virtue without gaining the other which he
sought in compensation. He lost not only his dominant lyrical
note, but also the ability to present a philosophical question in
terms which allowed him to preserve, and even to enrich, the
lyrical texture. What he had no doubt hoped to gain in compensation was the solid, hard, workaday technique in which
philosophical statement could be presented, stripped of its lyrical
garments.

The result seems occasional, awkward, and even arbitrary; nor
does the new workaday approach to language add anything in
the way of force and immediacy. It seems to me that he made
the mistake (natural enough in the circumstances) of trying his
hand at a direct presentation of thought, an immediate trans-

ference to poetry of his thought-processes, without the aid of
some dramatic or narrative framework. The result, as I have
said, is Teutonism rampant. And it is Teutonism without an
adequate symbolism. Pavlova dancing may be a focus for other
images and insights; rain may not.

The most interesting thing about these two poems, apart from
their transitional aspect, is that they are 'serious' in a way in
which the lyrics were not. In them, naïve rebelliousness yields
to the serious posing of a serious question; and their themes have
something in common with – indeed, they reflect – the philosophical puzzlement of the ordinary man. FitzGerald is no
longer setting himself apart; he has become a representative of
his fellows, however little he may have intended to do so. 'The
Hidden Bole', even though it is Romanticism bare and unashamed, is more *human* than all save four or five of the lyrics.

Since 'Essay on Memory', the poet's interest has shifted even
further. Now he is a licensed, fully-accredited dramatic poet.
'Heemskerck Shoals' and 'Fifth Day' have a blending of thought
with the narrative and dramatic; he is still concerned with the
themes of change and growth, with the backwardness of time;
but now he locates these themes in the field of human endeavour,
whether the endeavour be a success or a failure. The form of
the poems is more dramatic, and the tone more impersonal than
those of the earlier long poems. FitzGerald is not tortured any
longer by philosophical problems which have a direct, immediate
relevance to his own life. Consequently, the thoughts are more
leisurely and general, the development of each poem is more
like the development of an ordinary man's musings, and less
like that of a Shakespearian soliloquy spoken through a blurred
microphone at the wrong moment.

'Heemskerck Shoals' is an extraordinarily tedious poem for a
major Australian poet to have produced. But it does have one
or two pieces of poetry in it, and it does show the direction of
FitzGerald's thought. It deals with one of the voyages of Abel
Tasman, and takes us through a list of the major and minor
obstacles with which that explorer was faced, reaching at last
a sort of manifesto which is intended to belong to Tasman, but
which may also be taken as representing the thought of Fitz-
Gerald himself:

          Though that
was what the thought in his mind was biting at:
the necessity in men, deep down, close cramped,
not seen in their own hearts, for some attempt
at being more than ordinary men,
rising above themselves. It was an urge
that swung from wars to follies, being the purge
of stagnation from the veins, and violent when
there was little to work it off against; but was
man's only greatness also. Then, because
room hungered there for greatness, gaped in demand,
men could give greatness gladly to that land.

'That land' is, of course, Australia. The poem meanders prosily
along with more of the same kind of sentiment and reflection;
and it is not, all in all, a very profound or inspiring message.
One feels impelled to murmur: 'Monstrous! But one penny-
worth of thought to such an intolerable deal of prose.'

The 'Fifth Day', however, is a much more impressive conception, in all its parts and aspects. This deals with the fifth
day of the trial of Warren Hastings; and, unlike 'Heemskerck Shoals', it is not a third-person dramatic monologue. It
is rather like the first scene of a film scenario, written in verse.
We see Hastings, the victim; Edmund Burke, the prosecutor;
Francis, the informant; the two Houses of Parliament assembled;
the fashionable onlookers, eaten with curiosity. We see all this,
now through the eyes of FitzGerald, now through the eyes of
Joseph Gurney, a clerk whose only part in the proceedings is to
record them, and who is quite relieved when Burke collapses
under the strain, because it gives him the opportunity to go
home early.

Again, the theme is that of the continuity of human experience. But now it is played with variations. Every man, says
FitzGerald, is responsible for the actions of all his fellow men:

'Charges of misdemeanours and high crimes' –
prove – if proved, share them! Long ago, far hence,
they are drowned under the influx of new times.
What's done goes on for ever as consequence;
but there's some blurring of evidence
by happenings more at elbow. Why try this man?
Hastings is no concern of Pakistan.

> But it concerns all men that what they do
> remains significant unbroken thread
> of the fabric of our living. A man spoke so,
> and acted so; and everything done or said
> is superseded and overlaid
> by change of time and pattern. Be that as it may,
> there was need he lift his finger, say his say.

Men are actors in the drama of life, and so 'Attitude matters; bearing'. It is only by the recorded gesture and pose that we can assess events which have long ago become part of the stream of time. The changing fortunes of men are insignificant compared with the revealing externals which Joseph Gurney's pen, the witless instrument of the disinterested paid scribe, can record for us:

> Results mean little; they cancel and coalesce.
> A gesture will outweigh them, a trick of dress.

In such a view of life as this, the hero is not any one man, but mankind. The presumptive hero, be he Hastings or Burke, is there to endure for the sake of posterity; it is not his role to triumph:

> The axle's part
> is just to endure the play and spin of the spokes.

There is no dichotomy, in Eliot's terms, between acting and suffering. To act is to endure the rigours of one's representative role in time.

'Fifth Day' is a very intelligent, beautifully balanced, and mature poem. One would understand, however, if the bulk of modern readers found it arid and boring; its value is not guaranteed by any staple in their reading; it is, in fact, a completely new mode in contemporary poetry. FitzGerald's theme has not really changed, except in depth and complexity. His basic method, however, has altered entirely. In poems such as the ones I have already mentioned, as in 'Transaction', and the epic 'Between Two Tides', he is concerned with a poetry of statement, a poetry of ideas; and his method is to take an historical character, place him in some imaginative context which has possibilities for his dramatic development and, by analysing either his own thoughts or FitzGerald's comments on him, to show the philosophical significance of the adventure in which he is engaged. It is, as I have said, a quite new method. The modern poets, Pound and Eliot for example, who have attempted to extend our conception of drama in short poems have done nothing like it. Nor has any Australian poet, with the exception of Francis Webb, who probably learnt much of his technique from FitzGerald in any case. The nearest parallel is with Browning, a poet who shares much of his joyful, realistic spirit with FitzGerald. Yet even Browning has contributed little, if indeed he has contributed anything save personal example, to 'Fifth Day' and 'Transaction'. These two poems give us a Browning in a strict metrical pattern, a more visually exact Browning, a Browning whose tendency to diffuse his mental energies through a range of musings is disciplined to the needs of a statement clearly understood and deftly balanced. It is, in other words, a Browning completely translated; and so, no Browning at all.

Each poem is not only an experience of the poet's mind, but a courageous and imaginative grappling with a problem of technique. I have heard FitzGerald criticize a brother-poet on the grounds that he has never tackled a technical problem in his life. That is a charge to which many of us must plead guilty, with a repentance lessened in no way by the fact that the precise meaning of the charge is uncertain. At any rate, nobody could reasonably say it of FitzGerald himself. It is apparent that, over the last decade, he has seen each new creative opportunity not merely as a challenge to communicate a thought, but as a formal end to be achieved, and requiring the adaptation of new formal means. So he sees each poem as a problem; and each problem is different, in certain important respects, from the one which immediately preceded it. Yet we cannot fail to see, in addition, how continuous they are with one another – how 'Essay on Memory' leads on to 'Heemskerck Shoals', how 'Heemskerck Shoals' demands 'Fifth Day', and how this in turn provides the opportunity which is seized in 'Transaction' and, most important of all, in 'Between Two Tides'. The reader's interest is still in ideas, but it is an interest excited through the sheer control of form. The poet's interest, on the other hand, has been in making ideas formal, in arresting them in intricate shapes or cadences. This increasing and mature impersonality, this capacity to be excited by poetry as an objective form, has helped to save FitzGerald from the results of his earlier addiction to that kind of adolescent anarchism which may be called 'Lindsayism'.

'Between Two Tides' is his last long poem, though when it was actually written I have no idea. It is a work of epic proportions, impressive not only in its length (after all, 'The Great South Land' has it by the beard for size alone), but in the quality of its sustained thought. Once again, it is a work on the relationship between individuals and the past, security and the spiritual need for adventure, the stable, realized moment and the all-bearing flux. But it is a large work, a book as well as a poem. To give an account of it without estimating its value would be cowardice; to estimate its value without giving an account of it would be injustice; and I have leisure for an article, not a monograph.[1] All that it is necessary to say is that, if FitzGerald's place in our poetry were to be assessed by this poem alone, it would be a big, though not a pre-eminent one.

These brief notes show something of what has happened to FitzGerald's talent during its development. It may be as well to recapitulate. We find in the early short poems a struggle (sometimes causing great confusion of detail) between his lyrical impulse and his desire to elaborate general ideas. Later we see the lyrical impulse becoming subordinate to a philosophical end – in 'The Hidden Bole', strengthening and forming its ideas, in 'Essay on Memory' being destroyed by their undisciplined imperatives. Later still there is a further elimination of the lyrical note, until we have in the dramatic poems an austere realism, a philosophical realism which is, nevertheless, sometimes strangely graceful. It may be remarked that he still occasionally pens a lyric to keep his wrist supple; but these short pieces, where they are successful, exist in a style of calm and leisurely comment which is no doubt the result of his work in more dramatic modes. It is a fireside lyricism, or a lyricism of garden reflections, rather than of the clash of elemental forces.

An account of FitzGerald's development does not exhaust the critical possibilities of his poetry. Certain things are common to all stages of his development. He is, for example, an

[1] My view of it has been stated, however, in *Austrovert*.

'intellectual poet'; and this strain, whatever we mean by the title which is usually attached to it, is basic to his work. He is an intellectual; that is, he thinks, and the process of his thought is discernible, is traced, in his poetry. Yet more than this is necessary if the term is to have any commendatory meaning. I should call that poet intellectual who uses poetic form for the purpose of saying something, and of working out in his poetry the implications of that idea; and who uses his intellectual power to give clarity and distinctness to forms which have been made to bear such a burden of interpretation.

A good deal of nonsense is talked about FitzGerald's metaphysical complexity and intensity. It is doubtful whether he has ever read Donne, at least very closely; and it is equally doubtful whether he has ever been in the least attracted by Hopkins. In his best work, he certainly complies with the definition I have given of an intellectual poet. Yet I do not think that there is to be found anywhere in his work the painstaking analysis of a single mental state which is so recurrent a feature of Donne's poetry. There is, instead, either personal emotion formalized or general statement elaborated and dramatized; sometimes there are both together. There is never anything more detailed and exact. And, after all, it would be foolish to expect anything more. He is not an introspective poet, fascinated by his own sheer interiority; he is, if anything, a poet of action. Ideas in his work are given something of the quality of action; that is why they conduce so readily to dramatic treatment. And he seems interested in men not as incurably individual entities, but as fascinating examples. The impression of activity is everywhere in his work. We find there lots of sunlight, plenty of movement and life – and almost no brilliant colour at all. We do get an impression of greens and browns, but very seldom anything stronger or more striking. This may have a good deal to do with his profession as a surveyor. It may be that the nature of his work has caused him to turn to Nature for details of form and movement rather than of colour and surface life. There is, in the best and most forceful of his lyrics, an insistence upon transmitting the exact *feeling* of a movement which is at once clear-cut and angular:

> hawks hung in the wind above that verge
> where all falls bottomless and is nought,
> whence the tomorrows shall emerge
> which yet are cloudy and unwrought.
>
> Poised at time's focus on strong wings,
> like birds turned· sharply into the gust,
> your kisses have linked me to wise things
> saner than envy or distrust:

The delineation of the bird's action is clear and striking enough.
But FitzGerald goes on, and in the next stanza there is a change
in the imagery, without, however, a change in the emphasis on
effort and movement:

> Space for this moment is not more
> than a swollen raindrop, which could burst
> here at my lips and spill its store
> of riches on my clamouring thirst;
>
> and Now, holding its breath, reveals
> how each new summer like saved wine
> treasures old summer, and conceals
> springs yet ungathered, and all mine.

A closer look at these two stanzas will show to what extent he
is relying on images of movement to gain his effect of strength
and immediacy. The operative words are all of such a kind.
Space is a *'swollen* raindrop'; the raindrop *'bursts'* and *'spills'* its
riches; the poet's thirst is a *'clamouring'* one. The second of the
two stanzas is in a quieter tone; but we cannot help noticing
how the present moment, the 'Now', is represented as 'holding
its breath' — nothing less dramatic than that. The final effect of
this kind of imagery is of a great masculinity.

There are other elements in the poetry, besides a use of images
directly suggesting power, which contribute to this effect. For
example, there is the frequent use of verb-parts as adjectives, a
use which energizes the verse in a subtle way. We have 'the
pelting floodlight of the sun' — a most forceful way of giving us
the effect of summer sunlight in Australia. There is, too, the
use of words in an unusual and imaginative combination. The
linking of 'floodlight' and 'sun' in the phrase I have just quoted
would be one good example; other examples are to be found in
abundance.

The final element in the gaining of force and masculinity is simply a habit of phrasing. It is found to great effect in the eleventh poem in the 'Moonlight Acre' series:

> The fall of evening is the rebirth of knowing:
>
> it is then the body looks up and is not alone;
> for an old thought mingled with a newer thought
> swells, breaks the dam and sets the whole tide flowing.
>
> The tropic light over the sugarcane
> was weary daylong; and the eyes only sought
> to escape its colour, running from tuft to tuft;
>
> but with evening a lost eagerness we regain
> and watch how yellow of sunset will impress
> its strength upon native green, how the green, rebuffed,
>
> climbs helter-skelter to palm-tops, where they stoop,
> weighed under feather-branches, their headdress.
> All day though body walked upright, mind lay numb;
>
> but as in the cool the gathering shadows group
> so now some energies return from straying.
> Back to our startled universe they come
>
> and have zest for listening, seeing and marking down —
> but yonder a song and a ukulele playing:
> island airs sing in the heart its bitter truth . . .
>
> It is easier to let vague longings possess their own,
> stretch and relax, though almost we knew some urge
> to take up again the dropped threads of our youth.

This poem, which I have quoted in full, provides us with examples of all the various uses of language which make Fitz-Gerald a strong and distinctive poet — a poet of life and movement. In order to see just what is contributed by the element which I have loosely called 'phrasing', we may compare the impression of lassitude got from

> The tropic light over the sugarcane
> was *weary daylong*

with the impression of tenseness found in

> All day though body walked upright, mind lay numb,

and of renewed life in

Back to our startled universe they come
and have zest for listening . . .

We can see from all this that FitzGerald is not an inventive poet in the sense in which Auden, say, or MacNeice, is an inventive poet. He does not invent his own verse forms, as *they* occasionally do – nor does he revive old forms, such as the eclogue, for specifically modern purposes. On the contrary, his tendency is always toward the traditional fixed forms, or toward variations on them. His only real idiosyncrasy in this respect is his use of the alexandrine, a six-beat line, in certain poems; this is a measure taken over from Christopher Brennan in the period when he was 'imitating Brennan like mad'.

Nor does he *invent* images; despite a certain likeness to the metaphysicals, he has no liking for the metaphysical conceit. When we find a startling image in FitzGerald, it is startling only because the natural imagery on which he draws, the imagery of the Australian or Fijian landscape, is in itself sometimes surprising or, alternatively, it is startling because it comes at the end of a chain of images and to a certain extent punches home the last link in the chain.

From what I have been saying, it may be apparent that the titles of 'modernist' and 'intellectual' which are often applied to FitzGerald do not, at least in the sense intended for them, suit him at all. If he deserves our full and sympathetic attention, it is for other reasons than those derived from his supposed pioneering.

I have remarked that his is an impressionistic poetry; and such a judgment, stated so baldly, may itself be considered unduly impressionistic. Certainly his early lyrics work through impressions created by an accumulation of detail. But although the detail itself is often confused and inexact in its total effect, the outline of his poems, their external shape and movement, is generally firm and clear-cut. He is too active a poet to be summed up in the impressionistic formula; and his later poetry is, in any case, impressionist in a different and more satisfying sense. In 'Fifth Day', for example, the material detail is carefully selected and arranged to give an impression of drama just reaching its climax, its point of self-revelation. This use, in itself, shows an undeniable development.

What is true of his use of imagery is true also of his attitudes. He is too active a poet to have remained permanently under the spell of a Romantic vitalism, with all its emotionalism and aberration. We cannot fail to see in his later work (what is obscured in his earlier) a concern for the value of human life; and this is a concern which his explicit ideas, even as they are stated in the poems themselves, cannot thwart or undermine. His, which may be called poetry in action (though hardly a poetry *of* action), shows us something of our own human powers; at the same time, and without undue melancholy or contempt, it shows us something of the limitations of those powers.

His strain of Realist sympathy obviously has much to do with his use of the Australian landscape. I have made some comment on this, but must say more. You do not get the impression from his work, as too often you do with Judith Wright, that the Australian landscape is something to be feared, a force to be placated, either with blood or with lesser sacrifices. Whatever his philosophical attachment to vitalism or any other fluxive theory, the outline of his poetry shows little sign of its influence. His view of nature is firm and stable; his characteristic landscape is one of strong-thewed shapes, of firm yet challenging figures. He speaks often of nature in resounding tones; his familiarity with her is not of the sort which breeds contempt, but of a healthy respect and positive sympathy. He has become over the years more and more a visual realist.

All of these influences have made of his earlier naïve Romanticism a spur to dramatic poetry, and have so humanized it. His output shows that poetry for him is a genuine *habitus*, a central vocation. Yet only a fraction of it, I think, will retain a permanent value; and it is both idle and cruel to suggest that we have found in him that mythical monster, our Great Australian Poet.

A. D. Hope: The Unknown Poet

ALEC DERWENT HOPE is widely known in Australia as a public literary nuisance, a satirist, a critic, and a poet – very much in that order. The essay which follows will be concerned, among other things, to eliminate the first of these categories, and to put the remaining three into reverse order. Hope, of course, is a literary nuisance only to those literary men who most deserve to be disturbed, and who have greatest reason to fear a disturbance. And when a man is a good, genuine, and individual poet, one does not want to spend much time in writing about his criticism, or his verse attacks on social folly; such things are merely by-products of a life devoted to deeper values; in an essay as short as this, they can be disposed of with the briefest of references.

I am convinced that Hope is one of the three or four best living Australian poets, and our most discriminating living critic. I should like to state this conviction so firmly early in the piece, in order to remove any contrary impression which may be given when I come to deal with certain aspects of his work.

Despite the fact that he is a man of middle-age, his first book, *The Wandering Islands,* has only lately appeared. This fact largely justifies the scanty amount of attention his work has so far received; yet it does not entirely excuse the lack of understanding which has attended the infrequent references to it. For Hope had published quite enough of his best poetry to enable us to see of what spirit and of what stature he is. It is therefore all the more surprising to find a sympathetic surveyor such as Mr H. M. Green summing up his achievement in the following words:

> Equally savage in his disillusion . . . is Alec Hope, who has not yet collected his poems in book-form. To Hope, man is a vulgar and absurd little exhibitionist, who seeks release from a trivial and monotonous world in radio burble and comic adventure strip. His main preoccupation is with sexual love, and he sees life from somewhat of a Swiftian point of view.[1]

[1] *Australian Literature,* 1900-50 (M.U.P., 1951), p. 20.

To Hope, I should suggest, man is nothing of the kind; Mr
Green's remark is based on one satirical poem, and that not a
very good one. But if *his* judgment is surprising, it is infuriating
to see him taken to task, by Mr Macartney, for including Hope
at all in a survey of modern Australian literature. Here is Mr
Macartney:

> Mr Green provides an unusual example of this [that is, of
> 'special personal or localized knowledge or associations' to use
> the protesting critic's own words], by including in a summary of
> a country's literature a little-known poet represented in his
> 'Select Bibliography' by the rather anomalous words 'Verse
> uncollected'.[2]

This is a fantastic piece of shallow prejudice, for the committal
of which Hope himself is, unfortunately, in part responsible.
Nevertheless, enough of Hope's best poetry was available to the
practising critic to enable a more informed judgment than this.

The volume as a whole, when one leafs through it, surprises
one with the body of strength it displays. One's first, and admittedly rather startled impression is of a relatively small output,
small in comparison with the output of R. D. FitzGerald and
Judith Wright, yet of an extremely solid sort. The impression
is one of genuine poetic substance, of a sort of internal intactness
and strength in Hope's poetic achievement. And one's second
impression is that the solidity of the achievement itself rests
directly on a firmly held and consistent view of human experience, a view which has its exact corollary in Hope's view of poetic
form.

Yet both views, taken together, provide a mental idiom, a
mental world, unfamiliar to most people. It is an idiom of such
a kind that members of the *avant-garde* may feel impelled to
dismiss Hope as an incurable traditionalist, while people themselves incurably conservative (rather than traditionalist) may
regard him as an experimentalist, a confirmed tamperer with
the emotional *status quo*. The moralist may regard him as
amoral, the aesthete may find him distressingly didactic. A
recent reviewer or polemicist in the Sydney *Bulletin* has called
him an 'academic poet', although his poetry bears little resemblance to the academic writings of my acquaintance.

[2] *Meanjin*, Summer, 1951, vol. x, no. 4, p. 409.

Well, *sic transit* . . . and I suppose that, for this very reason,
I had better consider first his view and use of poetic form, in the
hope of saying enough about the nature of his poetic sensibility
to establish a context in which other elements of his mind and
his sensibility can be sympathetically considered.

Hope is usually called an 'intellectual poet'; and it would be
well to discuss what this word can possibly mean in terms of his
actual poetry. Certainly, as I shall suggest later, his satire is
that of an intellectual rather than of a superficially educated
man with a set of personal grievances. But his more 'lyrical'
poetry is the more important; and here we find nothing of philosophical argument given a tortuous poetic dress. In this sense,
Hope is not a 'philosophical poet'. Really intelligent poets rarely
are. One mistakes the nature of Brennan's poetry, for example,
if one thinks that it is concerned with working out philosophical
arguments. His esoteric symbolism may be a sign of intellectual
force and of deep convictions about intellectual values, but it is
not in itself argument, it does not work philosophically. Fitz-
Gerald and Browning are argufying poets. Brennan is not; nor
is Hope. In his poetry, ideas become images and symbols, the
sequences of argument become patterns of deed and perception.

> This is their image: the desert and the wild,
> A lone man digging, a nation piling stones
> Under the lash in fear, in sweat, in haste;
> Image of those demonic minds who build
> To outlast time, spend life to house old bones –
> This pyramid rising squarely in the waste!
>
> I think of the great work, its secret lost;
> The solid, blind, invincible masonry
> Still challenges the heart. Neglect and greed
> Have left it void and ruin; sun and frost
> Fret it away; yet, all foretold, I see
> The builder answering: 'Let the work proceed!'
>
> I think of how the work was hurried on:
> Those terrible souls, the Pharaohs, those great Kings
> Taking, like genius, their prerogative
> Of blood, mind, treasure: 'Tomorrow I shall be gone;
> If you lack slaves, make war! The measure of things
> Is man, and I of men. By this you live.'

This is without doubt a very satisfying poetry, and yet it does not argue a case, it simply creates a pattern of ineluctably solid things and images in which two or more varying conceptions of human permanence are brought together and allied. We feel in poetry of this kind the constant play and impact of a mind revolving the profound issues of its own existence – but objectifying them, spinning them away from the smaller world where 'discussion' takes place. The revolutions of the wheeling mind are finished by the time the poetry begins; all that is left is its vibration, and of that vibration poetry comes, not further argument.

The poem itself, like all of Hope's best poems, presupposes a philosophical argument which has already taken place, and which here has its reverberations – its consolidation and completion – in attitude and phrasing. To my mind, it is a conception much more sophisticated than that of, say, R. D. FitzGerald, whose poetry, at its most 'philosophical', tends to become something of a platform on which to raise the issues of his own necessarily half-formulated conceptions.

I do not want to give a false impression of Hope; and this is always a present danger when one is concerned to dispel a false impression of a different sort. He is, after all, an extremely reflective poet, and his poetry *is,* among other things, a way of clarifying for himself the issues which he finds most important in life. Yet it would be a mistake to see him as a clever, abstruse man whose poetry is (like that of so many modern poets) a substitute for something else, for other disciplines in which he ought, by rights, to engage separately.

There is another fact, too; Hope's intellectual vigour and competence may be seen in his attitude to, and control of, poetic forms as such:

> Here are the weaving branches
> Of that resplendent eye,
> The rivers' wandering trenches
> Left when the rivers dry.
>
> And through the blank of summer
> Their parching channels spread;
> The last pools steam and shimmer;
> The reeds are brown and dead.

> For you are both the season
> That brimmed their banks with rain
> And the blind, wasting passion
> That dries them out again.
>
> The eye, whose large horizons
> Were quick with liquid sight,
> Now circles in your prison's
> Impenetrable light.

The approach to form here may be called syllogistic. The natural scene is set, simply and neatly, before its analogy with the human situation is stated; and both things are indicated with a complete sense of and attention to what we ought, I suppose, to call their inner logic. The dried summer river-bed is like an eye, but it is also a river-bed; and it is evoked in terms appropriate to a river-bed before the conceit is taken up once more and extended. In this way, the extension of the conceit is seen to follow logically (and I am sure that Hope himself would add 'naturally') from the description of nature.

Yet the language of logic and syllogistic form may be misleading. It is not simply a question of his working out a thought in his poetry, and presenting the premises before the conclusion to be derived from them. It is rather a question of his having brought image and idea into a relationship of such a kind that the completion of the one can be accomplished only with the proper working out of the other. The terms in which the idea is imaged determine the extent to which it is to be developed as an idea; and in developing it, Hope is intent on developing image and idea *together*, making them complementary and mutually expressive.

The point I am making is one difficult to grasp unless it is fully illustrated; and that is a task involving many pages. It may help matters, however, if I add that many of Hope's poems are concerned with objective situations, and that he imposes his logical order on them by making them as much like events as possible. We see the use of such a method in 'Imperial Adam', a poem which has an ironic twist in the last line, but which pays attention to other human realities besides the paradoxical way in which joy seems to beget horror. In evoking the atmosphere of the garden of Eden, Hope treats the situation of Adam and

Eve not as a mere piece of symbolism, but as a set of events;
and he uses his poetic form to give those events the kind of
logical sequence which events must have if they are to be
properly understood:

> From all the beasts, whose pleasant task it was
> In Eden to increase and multiply
>
> Adam had learned the jolly deed of kind:
> He took her in his arms and there and then,
> Like the clean beasts, embracing from behind,
> Began in joy to found the breed of men.
>
> Then from the spurt of seed within her broke
> Her terrible and triumphant female cry,
> Split upward by the sexual lightning stroke.
> It was the beasts now who stood watching by:
>
> The gravid elephant, the calving hind,
> The breeding bitch, the she-ape big with young
> Were the first gentle midwives of mankind;
> The teeming lioness rasped her with her tongue;
>
> The proud vicuña nuzzled her as she slept
> Lax on the grass; and Adam watching too,
> Saw how her dumb breasts at their ripening wept,
> The great pod of her belly swelled and grew,
>
> And saw its water break, and saw, in fear,
> Its quaking muscles in the act of birth,
> Between her legs a pigmy face appear
> And the first murderer lay upon the earth.

In its combination of strong formal control, rich sensuous
perception, and extremely precise diction, this is remarkable
among modern poetry. There is no need to defend my statement
about its chief qualities. It has the air of passionate and most
pointed utterance avoiding rhetoric by a sheer control of form;
and that control is achieved, as I have been insisting, by treating
the poem's situation as a sequence of events, and giving them
the authority not only of the author's manner but also of their
own strong logic.

It is not always so in Hope's poetry. The poems from which
I have already quoted are among those in his later period.

Many readers are likely to be puzzled, however, at some of his
earlier poetry which, despite a superficial resemblance in form
to the later, lacks precisely those virtues which are so com-
pellingly displayed in the later:

> She did not see them there, the four men, all
> Wound in her arms, sharing his startled eyes:
> Cocksure the Great Seducer crowed his song;
> The virile bristles rustled down his thighs;
> The golden feathers sprouted from his tail;
> His heart's bronze warders smacked their mighty gong.
>
> But the Slave's heart, in that tremendous din,
> Burst counting the incredible troops of lust.
> Her Old Boy's Union, with beer and hearty jokes,
> Held celebrations, invited him to join,
> Published their names in alphabetical lists,
> Danced round the bonfire of his burning sex.
>
> The Observer landed, smiling, from his yacht,
> Notebook in hand, rubbed noses with the chief.
> 'The native girl's magnificent physique
> Makes her insatiable in love', he wrote.
> The surf ran moaning on the jagged reef.
> His camera gave the customary click.

Sex again! But this time a lack of properly poetic control over
its implications. Hope is trying here to play the detached
observer of life and love, and is, in a way, giving insufficient
attention to the development of his poem. Its point is clear
enough: It is that, in the act of sexual love, each man plays the
various (and in some sense, contradictory) roles of Great Seducer,
Slave, scientific Observer, and true Lover. It is a point quite in
keeping with Hope's practice as a satirist. But, even though it
is a clear point, it is not a sufficiently sharp one. What blunts
it is the ambiguous tone, wavering between exultation and
cynicism, the mixture of styles, and the imitation of certain of
the fashionable poets of the thirties. It is all difficult and a little
off-key, hard to get in touch with; too many strains and images
are linked together, not perhaps by violence (or, at any rate, not
a wanton violence), but at least by a certain obsessional force.
There is something even of sentimentalism about an ambiguity
of this kind.

But we are interested mainly in Hope at his best; and Hope at his best is a poet as unusual in achievement as he is positive in statement. We find in his work, what is surely an unusual thing for an Australian poet, a highly developed tactile sense, a sense of our actually touching things, or of being touched by them. In most Australian poetry, the tactile tends to give way to the visual sense; there is usually a facile music, a thinning of the sense, a certain evidence that eyes accustomed to long and distant horizons do not readily see things in such an immediate way that they are brought present to the sense of touch as well. With Hope it is different, and he is almost alone among Australian poets in the degree to which his tactile sense dominates the other senses and directs his mind. We see this merely in one of the lines from the piece I have just quoted:

The virile bristles rustled down his thighs.

We find as well a marching line, a line which tends towards weighty and rhythmic utterance rather than to the lilt or the cadenced involutions of verbal dance. There is nothing of chant about his work, and little of song. This preference is quite in keeping with his attitude to form, and any other kind of music would probably tend to the dissolution of his form rather than to its firmer establishment. After all, he is not a deliberate self-expressionist; in fact, he avoids expressionist poetry as far as he can. He *does* express his own inner states, and in his earlier poetry he does so in a rather compulsive manner; but he does so mostly by the way, as a necessary part of the attempt to do something else. This is largely the reason for his eschewing a lyrical form and a lyrical manner. Even the lovely lyric 'Now the heart sings' has its lilt firmly controlled to bring it into the pattern of an exact statement:

Now the heart sings with all its thousand voices
To hear this city of cells, my body, sing.
The tree through the stiff clay at long last forces
Its thin strong roots and taps the secret spring.

In other words, Hope is a classical poet whose material is Romantic; it is not possible to give a glib definition of those terms; I am relying on the probability that their meaning will be instinctively recognized. He absorbs the world in terms of a

sensibility which is unusual, individualistic, even at times un-
balanced and anarchistic; but, that world once part of him, it is
subjected to the judgment, to the formative influence, of a
strong, deliberate, rather heavy mind. I shall be saying more
about the way in which he sees the world. Here I may simply
add that, in the poetic event, he gives us a poetry in which the
tension between his mind and emotions does not issue, as we
might have expected it to issue, in an investigation of his own
states of mind, but in an arrangement of deeds and symbols.
The 'classical' control of form, its syllogistic bent, is Hope's way
of making fully objective, of removing from himself, his own
tensions and preoccupations. More than any other Australian
poet of the present day, the nature of his preoccupations
demands that he put them into perspective. A classical form is
his way of doing this; and so we get a poetry which is implicitly
dramatic, but never explicitly so, either in its form or in its
methods of investigation.

McAuley too is a classical poet in something the same sense.
Yet Hope's poetry is much less lyrical, much less supple and
subjective, than his. The reason is that Hope's poetry derives
more directly than McAuley's from his own preoccupations (I
had almost said, his own obsessions), and his more rigid use of
form is a creative reaction to that fact. Certainly, it enables him
to do things, to achieve effects, which no other Australian poet
can do or achieve. One may paraphrase somebody else in saying :
'If Hope did not exist, it would be necessary to invent him'.

We have, then, a heavy almost brooding mind consciously
detaching itself in the act of poetry from what most exercises
and torments it. This gives readily enough an impression of
complete objectivity which is by no means in accordance with
the facts. Certainly, it seems to be the explanation for his writing
so much satirical poetry, and satirical poetry of such a kind.

I had better make it clear that I neither like most of Hope's
satire nor consider it important. It is true that it does not express
either shallow criticisms of unimportant social follies or personal
grievances; it is true, too, that it is directed against men who fail,
for one reason or another, to achieve their full human stature.
or who try to overshoot the bounds of their own nature and
possibilities. Yet in their actual working-out, such poems as 'The

Return from the Freudian Islands', 'The Brides', and 'Helden-sagen' themselves overshoot their mark, and express a revulsion disproportionate to the follies which they attack. They are, in general, too much and too flamboyantly coloured by Hope's personal worries. Only in such a work as 'Dunciad Minimus', part of which was published in 1950 in *Melbourne University Magazine*, does the true satirical note fully emerge and claim our sympathy. I suppose it emerges too in 'Easter Hymn', which is, in any case, only partly a satire:

> The City of God is built like other cities:
> Judas negotiates the loans you float;
> You will meet Caiaphas upon committees;
> You will be glad of Pilate's casting vote.
>
> Your truest lovers still the foolish virgins,
> Your heart will sicken at the marriage feasts
> Knowing they watch you from the darkened gardens
> Being polite to your official guests.

The anger and its cause are glimpsed through a dissolving haze of good humour, or at least a tinge of playfulness. At its occasional best, this kind of satirical verse manages to effect a balance between condemnation and genuine amusement, be-tween the compulsive and the light-hearted. One gets the im-pression that Hope uses satire partly as a safety-valve, partly as a means of objective comment, and partly as a game. When the first of these predominates (as it too often does) we get un-balanced satire, a statement of revulsion which itself comes to seem repulsive, the suggestion that a God's eye view is being taken of the human situation. And this we cannot allow; we cannot defer to a criticism of human folly which goes so far as to express disgust with life itself, and to condemn, by defacing it, the human image. Perhaps, with Hope, the process does not often go as far as this; but it approaches it too often. The quality in him which goes to mar some of his other poetry operates in his satire by reaction. And one feels that it is not only inferior as a genre, it is not the most suited to Hope's particular talent. There-fore, those critics who write in praise of his 'savage satire' do him an actual disservice. To allot such praise is really to administer a left-handed justice; and when it becomes the chief remark on his poetic achievement – the remark which every commentator feels obliged to make – it becomes something very much like lynch law, though it and its victim are executed, of course, with every kind intention.

When we consider Hope's typical attitudes and conceptions we see further evidence of something which I have been stressing throughout, of his savage subjectivism made objective, given a more general application, simply by a control of form. He is teaching us, in his own way, the lesson which Shelley and Coleridge, for example, unhappily failed to learn. At any rate, his love for the eighteenth century helps him to understand it, as they did not.

The subject is inevitably approached by considering Hope's emphasis on sex, which is one of the most controversial features of his work. For the sake of comment his poem 'Chorale' needs to be quoted in full:

Often had I found her fair;
Most when to my bed she came,
Naked as the moving air,
Slender, walking like a flame.
In that grace I sink and drown:
Opening like the liquid wave
To my touch she laid her down,
Drew me to her crystal cave.
    Love me ever, love me long –
    Was the burden of her song.

All divisions vanish there;
Now her eyes grow dark and still;
Now I feel the living air
With contending thunder fill;
Hear the shuddering cry begin,
Feel the heart leap in her breast,
And her moving loins within
Clasp their strong, rejoicing guest.
    Love me now, O now, O long!
    Is the burden of her song.

Now the wave recedes and dies;
Dancing fires descend the hill;
Blessed spirits from our eyes
Gaze in wonder and are still.
Yes our wondering spirits come

From their timeless anguish freed:
Yet within they hear the womb
Sighing for the wasted seed.
Love may not delay too long –
Is the burden of their song.

This is a forceful and lovely poem; there is no need to stress the fact that it is also a poem hymning sexual union, and doing so with unashamed lyricism. I have taken it for comment in order to anticipate and refute a criticism which will no doubt be made time and time again about Hope's poetry: that it is sexually obsessed, and obsessed in an unpleasant manner. It would be a mistake to regard this poem, for example (and it is perhaps the most explicit of his sexual poems) as *that* and no more. It would be ridiculous to regard it as pornography. It is true that the drama of the poem's development comes to its climax with the climax of the sexual act which provides its theme. But the total effect of the poem itself is to initiate us into a world in which sex is a representative, but by no means the only value, perhaps not even the dominant value. Sexual union is recognizably the theme, but the context of the whole poem is such that the union comes to *represent* more than it *is*. The world into which we are initiated is one in which the most intense quality of living and perception is presented through a pattern of images (of air, water, movement, light, and so on) which focus on and elevate sex itself. This is admittedly only one of Hope's poetic attitudes to sex, but it is the attitude expressed in his best poetry. We find it in 'Imperial Adam', too; there the solidity of the figures and the precision of the events seem to be surrounded by a width of dissolving light which gives them a significance greater than any which of themselves they possess. It is a technique similar to that of certain medieval painters; and in both cases the technique is the result of a definite attitude to life. 'The Damnation of Byron', probably Hope's best-known work, does not possess this very air and atmosphere; it is a world, rather, of sharp pictures and forceful moral judgment – a profoundly moral poem. Even so, the imaginative world which it presents is as expansive as that of 'Imperial Adam'.

The other sexual strain in his writing is less likeable; it is, in fact, extraordinarily unpleasant and disturbing at times. There is a recurrent bitter carnality, even a sort of bestiality (perhaps beastishness is a better word) discernible in Hope's work; and it is nearly always associated with sex. One of his poems is called 'Circe', and it is a very interesting piece of work; I mention it here only to say that, from a casual reading of his poems, one might gather the impression that he regards woman as being, of her nature, a Circe. Yet a closer inspection would show not only that Hope does not make any such suggestion but that it is a suggestion actually quite foreign to his most profound attitudes, to his concern with an order at once personal and cosmic.

The point is that his attitude to sex is intimately connected with his attitude to the physical world as such. His advanced tactile sense gives him an unusually, almost an abnormally, acute sense of the physical – of its contours and its relations, even of the feel of its inner biological life. And he is quite as conscious of decomposition and distortion as he is of the positive *being* which it contains. So we see him alternating between a controlled affirmation of the physical and a less firmly controlled revulsion from it. Sometimes his sense of physical corruption emerges so strongly that it goes over the edge of control into an almost Manichæan disgust. In 'Massacre of the Innocents', we find horror given its full carnal flavour in a statement which is barely held back from rhetoric by an anguished yet controlling hand :

> This is the classic painter's butcher shop;
> – Choice cuts from the Antique – Triumphant Mars
> Takes his revenge, the whistling falchions swoop
> Round Venus as the type of all mammas.

This will bear comparison with (say) 'Imperial Adam' because they are both 'objective' poems, both reworkings of well-known events, and both based on previous accounts of those events. This poem, for example, is a comment on a painting by Cornelius van Haarlem. Yet no matter how much Hope may disapprove of van Haarlem's excessive physicality, he is surely showing his own excess in the very act of protest. The bantering tone is quite ineffectual to conceal or laugh away the horror of (or, perhaps, the horrified attraction to) the physical with which the lines are laden.

The truth is that, almost alone among Australian poets since Brennan, Hope has a tragic dimension, which, however, his poetry reveals but imperfectly. When he exalts the passions, including the passion of thought, he does so in a finely controlled, 'eventful' rhetoric and in a beautifully physical way – very unlike McAuley's more graceful, more Irish gift. When he states the case *against* man's dignity, he does so in similar language, but in a poetically far less satisfying way. He is himself so much involved in the physical universe which merits variously his praise and condemnation that he has to make his poetry a means of distancing himself from that world. As I have suggested, it is when physical horror enters his consciousness that he fails most signally to do this.

There is more to it than that, of course. The world as Hope sees and presents it is a world of human beings rather than of natural objects. He is wedded to the idea of the primacy of the human, even while he is most intensely insistent on the final insufficiency of the human. He is not at all a political poet, as so many modern poets are; he sees man in a metaphysical dimension rather than a social one – and in a metaphysical dimension which seems to exclude the social as either irrelevant or unimportant. We could do with a little more of this sort of thing; and I am content to say so even though I do not share Hope's apparent disdain for the social life of man. This is a reaction against what the last two centuries have made of Renaissance humanism. It is, in some sense, a reaction against Renaissance values as such, even though Hope seems to me in many ways a type of Renaissance man. It would probably be truer to say that he is a type of eighteenth-century man, sharing with him an emphasis on the primacy of reason and an intense awareness of the physical universe, but differing from him in his belief that man is perfectible, that the world began with the reign of Queen Elizabeth I, and that society is a pleasant and necessary contract for the mutual protection of man. In other words, despite his emphasis on reason, Hope is not really a poet of the Enlightenment.

It is difficult, of course, to decide the dates of many of his poems; yet I feel little hesitation in saying that his later poetry (that in the section entitled 'Pyramis *or* The House of Ascent') is his best, as it is certainly his most 'classical'. We can see him on the whole gradually writing his way out of satire, out of a largely satirical approach to life, and gradually achieving a hard joy. He is beginning more and more to combine his deeply ironic qualities with a sense of the real value of persons and things, grasped and expressed in all their sensuous compactness. The early poetry, with its somewhat random experimental tendencies, is yielding to a poetry in which a consistent attempt is made to get a form more suited to Hope's 'classical' view of man and his destiny. He is giving mythology a modern twist, while preserving its traditional force and authority. At the same time, he has never ceased to put his own doubts and dilemmas into a comparatively rigid classical context in order at once to disguise them and to give them an added reverberation and a permanent solidity. One of the disturbing things about his total output is that, despite the increasing maturity of his verse, there is no corresponding increase in its fertility. It is an output in many ways too small for comfort. One senses a lack either of energy or of the more obvious kind of dedication to the art itself. And so, if we are to account for the feeling of solidity which we get about his work, we shall have to seek a different and more profound dedication.

I feel that Hope is a recognizably modern poet, in whom lyricism and satire combine and sharpen each other. In his best poems, his control of his material is of a remarkable order. I should hazard the guess that he came late to poetic maturity; there is consequently about him nothing of the precocious boy, still less of the garrulous one who is the prototype of so many modern poets. I should like to complete this analysis of his work – which is also, despite its occasional carping, something of a personal tribute to him – by quoting his poem on the death of W. B. Yeats:

> To have found at last that noble, candid speech
> In which all things worth saying may be said,
> Which, whether the mind asks, or the heart bids, to each
> Affords its daily bread:
>
> To have been afraid neither of lust nor hate,
> To have shown the dance, and when the dancer ceased,
> The bloody head of prophecy on a plate
> Borne in at Herod's feast;

To have loved the bitter, lucid mind of Swift,
Bred passion against the times, made wisdom strong;
To have sweetened with your pride's instinctive gift
The brutal mouth of song;

To have shared with Blake uncompromising scorn
For art grown smug and clever, shown your age
The virgin leading home the unicorn
And loosed his sacred rage —

But more than all, when from my arms she went
That blessed my body all night, naked and near,
And all was done, and order and content
Closed the Platonic Year,

Was it *not* chance alone that made us look
Into the glass of the Great Memory
And know the eternal moments, in your book,
That we had grown to be?

Some of the same things may be said of Hope himself. He
shares with Swift a passionate lucid mind, with Blake a sense of
reverence and uncompromising scorn, and is developing, as
Yeats did, a speech which may well be called candid and even
noble. Despite the puzzling crudities of much of his work, therefore, and despite the irregularity of his inspiration, we must insist
that he is a part of the new humanist tradition in Australian
poetry, of sophistication and depth working together. My
remarks on his work, if they are taken as being a just estimate,
should indicate what an important part of it he is.

The Poetry of Judith Wright

THE REPUTATION of being a poet, prophet, nature-lover, and true woman all together is one very difficult to sustain; and, if it is difficult to sustain, it is almost impossible to justify. The weight of uncritical adulation which has been heaped on the work of Judith Wright would surely have proved, to a lesser poet, quite destructive of his native talent; even in the case of such a good poet as Miss Wright, it is a burden which her poetry should not be required to bear.

There is evidence that it has already proved a distraction to her, that it has begun to harm her development. The false simplicity of accent in much of her latest book, *The Gateway*, the increasing impersonality, the hints of a growing portentousness, the assumption that what can be done once can be done without effort a dozen times – these are the signs of interior strain which the Australian critics, by their unthinking praise, have done as much as anybody else to cause. The innumerable distractions which, by her voluntary isolation, the poet had sought to escape have been foisted on her by her distant friends, and have become aggravated by that very isolation.

Yet she remains one of the few really good Australian poets now living; and the total body of her written works is a rich and glistening experience. What remains in her later work is the lyrical beauty, the cold brilliance, and the sense of artistic certainty; what is now missing is the excitement of the profoundly new, the sense of individual discovery, and the very human warmth.

One cannot help feeling that her first book, *The Moving Image*, was received with such acclaim because it dealt so directly with human problems and with the various life of the Australian landscape; the praise which was rightly given to her for that book has been increasingly distributed since the appearance of her second and third – and it has been based on the presumed existence of the same qualities, which are in fact no longer to be found in her poetry.

If we had to sum up her poetry in a formula (which God forbid) we might say that she is a modernist poet with a pronounced quasi-mystical bent, a new and somewhat apocalyptic attitude to nature, and an addiction to lyrical forms which are made to bear a dramatic emphasis. We might say so, and still be very far from making any genuinely positive judgment on her poetry; what such a formula enables us to do is to bring the various elements in her work into a proper relationship, and to avoid the risk of stressing any one of them to the exclusion of the others.

The question of her 'modernism' is soon settled; it could have been settled much sooner if her commentators had not persisted in confusing the appropriate categories. To call her a modernist is not to say that she is a markedly experimental poet; for she is not. Nor is it to bring her within the number of those whose approach has been dominated (and in some cases determined) by the psychological discoveries of the Surrealists; for she has very little to do with this tendency in modern poetry. She is an adherent neither of experimental formalism nor of the theories of 'organic form' which some writers inherited from the Surrealists. If these are the poles of modernism, then she is not a modernist at all. Yet she *is* a modern poet – a modernist in a somewhat different sense. The influences on her work alone demonstrate the contention. She is conventional in having been influenced first by the more imprecise features of Eliot's poetry, and later by the Blake of the neo-Romantic dream. She is modern in the duties of philosophical reflection and dramatic sharpness with which she burdens the lyrical form. She is modern in her obsession with time and with the means of overcoming it. She is modern in her reliance on image as a partial substitute for statement. And she is modern, finally, in her faint though recurrent tendency to make poetry do things, to complete states of being, which it is not traditionally equipped to do.

The lyrical element in her work, which is very strong, takes a typically modern form. It works through images which are used to give us a sensuous counterpart to the poet's ideas and emotions. Yet her conception of lyrical feeling, and her use of poetic forms to express it, do vary from book to book. Although her own brand of lyrical feeling dominates almost all the poems in *The Moving Image*, there is hardly a poem there which could be confidently called a lyric. The movement of these poems is lyrical, but the form is not. It would seem that, in this first book, Miss Wright is too preoccupied with images of the decay wrought by time to allow herself to find an appropriate lyrical form; consequently, the poems are less lyrics than statements, mediated through images, on certain themes or situations presented with a mixture of dramatic emphasis and lyrical feeling. In *Woman to Man*, with the access of a more joyful and spontaneous emotion, comes a new kind of lyricism; and it is accompanied, paradoxically enough, by a new and more satisfying quality of drama. The poems written on the birth of her child are surely the finest things she has done; certainly they are, in form and emotion alike, the most rounded and complete. In the poem 'Woman to Man', for example, the trilling emotion is carried down to its satisfying conclusion along a thread of subtly dramatic rises and falls, of haltings and accelerations. The emotion, the sense of urgency, are perfectly adapted to the verse-form:

> This is no child with a child's face;
> this has no name to name it by:
> yet you and I have known it well.
> This is our hunter and our chase,
> the third who lay in our embrace.
>
> This is the strength that your arm knows,
> the arc of flesh that is my breast,
> the precise crystals of our eyes.
> This is the blood's wild tree that grows
> the intricate and folded rose.
>
> This is the maker and the made;
> this is the question and reply;
> the blind head butting at the dark,
> the blaze of light along the blade.
> Oh hold me, for I am afraid.

But this lovely fusing of elements seems to have been fortuitous; for it has seldom happened since those half-dozen poems. The lyrical note in *The Gateway* is colder and slightly off-pitch, less related to a specific and recognizable situation, less firmly sustained by a personal emotion. The lyrics in this latest volume seem at first sight freer, closer to the conception of 'pure poetry' of which A. E. Housman was so disastrously fond. Yet they are freer in another sense as well; they waver and dip, their form is not clear-cut, their images on the whole are too arbitrary and too commonplace. They are, in fact, not true lyrics at all.

Has Judith Wright ever, indeed, written a true lyric? Probably not, if we are to judge lyrical form by the criteria of *The Golden Treasury*. If we call Miss Wright a lyrical poet (and I think we must) we shall have to be careful about the meaning of the term. For her, the lyric tends to be a compressed version of some other poetic form. And in this tendency, too, she is modern. The tradition of lyricism of which Burns is such a splendid example has almost no representatives in modern poetry. The reasons for this are not entirely creditable to modern society, nor entirely relevant to a brief study of Judith Wright; the fact itself is deplorable. But the lyrical impulse stubbornly persists, and she has a very considerable dose of it. She uses it, much as other modern lyrists do, in such a way that the simple impulse to sing becomes sublimated in image and allusion, rather than expressed directly in line-movement and phrasing. She is one of the best and most lyrical representatives of a self-conscious age.

The recurrent lyrical mood becomes a means by which she can envision man and nature. For, although she is not a mere 'nature-poet', natural processes are the central fact in her vision of the world, the source and standard to which everything else is referred.

I have said that she is not a 'mere nature-poet'. What I mean is that she is not primarily interested in describing nature, or in chronicling her own delighted responses to it. Anyone who has read the reviews of her books must have noticed that she is sometimes referred to as an 'intellectual poet'; and in the context of her actual poetry such a term seems almost meaningless. But she is more often mentioned as though her importance consisted in the fact that she deals with subjects of primarily feminine interest *or* in the fact that she enables us to see various elements in the Australian landscape in a fresh way. She is talked about, in other words, as though she were a highbrow Dorothy Dix or a new kind of that strange species of recorder, describer, rhapsodist, and impressionist, which we call a 'nature-poet'.

Such judgments, as applied to Miss Wright, are ridiculous.
Any one of her poems will show as much. 'Bora Ring' will
certainly do so:

> The song is gone; the dance
> is secret with the dancers in the earth,
> the ritual useless, and the tribal story
> lost in an alien tale.
>
> Only the grass stands up
> to mark the dancing-ring: the apple-gums
> posture and mime a past corroboree,
> murmur a broken chant.
>
> The hunter is gone: the spear
> is splintered underground; the painted bodies
> a dream the world breathed sleeping and forgot.
> The nomad feet are still.
>
> Only the rider's heart
> halts at a sightless shadow, an unsaid word
> that fastenes in the blood the ancient curse,
> the fear as old as Cain.

Such lines as

> the apple-gums
> posture and mime a past corroboree

have often been praised for the way in which they cast a new
light, the light of an individual vision, on an irregular line of
native trees. And she does in fact get such a freshness. Yet the
significance of these lines goes far beyond such imaginative
visual effects. They are a part of Judith Wright's lament for the
death of aboriginal civilization, a death which, as she insists, is
not merely grounds for a pleasantly romantic fancy, but which
has power to move to terror and dismay the heart of the white
man:

> Only the rider's heart
> halts at a sightless shadow, an unsaid word
> that fastens in the blood the ancient curse,
> the fear as old as Cain.

She is not precisely offering an indictment of our treatment of
the aborigines; that sort of complaint is not really in keeping
with her general attitude to poetry. Although the suggestion of
guilt and terror is unmistakably there, she is making a point
not so much about man's injustice to man as about the general

catastrophe of life in which the aboriginal cultures, like all others, have been implicated. Her concern is, in a way, a moral one, and it is a concern with the calamitous nature of life itself. This remains central to her early poetry even though the poem under discussion is a moving one on the level of an imaginative reconstruction of landscape; and we must insist that neither aspect of it can be separated from the other without damage to her talent and reputation.

At no stage of her development does Miss Wright play the part of a mere descriptive poet, no matter how forceful may be individual bits of description and evocation. We should, I think, be more concerned with the kind of attitude which makes evocation and description necessary, and with the terms in which they are done.

But she does seem to be a 'nature-poet' in another sense. For one thing, she draws her symbols from nature rather than from society; for another, she shows man's struggle with himself in terms of external nature, of natural things and events. And, above all, she consistently returns to the idea of nature as a powerful, animated force, against which man is powerless, and which will suck the life from men who do not co-operate with it – in other words, a sort of beautiful though petulant octopus. Little Josie is defeated by nature as much as by society; the three old people of 'Brother and Sisters' are impotent and neurotic in the face of the bush's implacable hostility; the once-friendly sea turns sour on the surfer; even the bullocky, with the sacred cachet of history affixed to his pioneering, is driven mad by the loneliness of the outback. One is constantly getting the suspicion that Miss Wright tends to think of nature in such terms as savages use – as something to be feared, even propitiated, as the main agent of destructive time. In all her books, the conception of nature which she advances is suspiciously close to a kind of sophisticated animism.

This strain is, at any rate, reasonably constant throughout her first book, and is to be found even in the second. *The Gateway*, however, reveals an inversion of the earlier values – an inversion which is not so complete as it may at first sight appear. In the latest poems, nature is seen as possessing a different kind of power, the power not of animistic force but of archetypal

symbols. Nature in the first case is a threat; in the second it is
a sort of gnostic script. But in both cases it is equally hypnotic,
equally transcendent, and even contemptuous, of ordinary
human life.

In 'The Moving Image' itself, she gives full rein to her
despair:

> Looking from so high the world is evil and small
> like a dried head from the islands with a grin of shell,
> brittle and easy to break. But there is no end to the breaking –
> one smashed, another mocks from your enemy's eye –
> put that out, there's a world in every skull.

In a much later poem, 'The Ancestors', she surrounds a similar
analysis with the glittering figures of a dream-landscape:

> Their slow roots spread in mud and stone,
> and in each notched trunk shaggy as an ape
> crouches the ancestor, the dark bent foetus,
> unopened eyes, face fixed in unexperienced sorrow,
> and body contorted in the fern-tree's shape.

Ten years separate these two visions; and although the
second seems more positive, more imbued with mystical awareness, the two visions are in the end only the one. It is only the
décor that has changed; nature herself is still the tyrant, over-
riding the stature of man and mocking his image of himself.
She has other aspects, of course: the almost human beauty of
pools and stars, the reflective and quasi-religious force of 'Lion'.
Yet we must not be deceived; 'nature-poetry' may still be the
opening to a private Inferno of the inward eye.

What remains of all this striving after the secret of nature
is probably not a vision of nature-in-general, but a sense of the
symbolic power of the particular landscapes of Australia. In some
of her moods or moments, Judith Wright surpasses all other
Australian poets in the extent to which she mediates the pressure,
and reveals the contours, of Australia as a place, an atmosphere,
a separate being. It is true that she does so largely by the way,
as a result or by-product of the pursuit of other preoccupations;
and at times the revelation is confused, obscured either by an
inordinate pessimism or by a lapse into private mythology. But
the achievement remains; it shows a positive side to her
responsiveness, an exciting gift of impressionist language, and a

sense of man's responsibility to the land. It is positive only when she ceases to insist on landscape as expressive of mystical qualities, and sees it as a thing, a context for human life.

She has a method of giving depth to her treatment of Australian scenes which sets her apart from most of her fellow-poets, and which makes doubly ridiculous the comment that she is mainly a conventional nature-poet. In order to see what this quality is, let me make another comparison. Here is Miss Wright's poem 'Bullocky', which is probably the best poem in *The Moving Image*:

> Beside his heavy-shouldered team,
> thirsty with drought and chilled with rain,
> he weathered all the striding years
> till they ran widdershins in his brain:
>
> Till the long solitary tracks
> etched deeper with each lurching load
> were populous before his eyes,
> and fiends and angels used his road.
>
> All the long straining journey grew
> a mad apocalyptic dream,
> and he old Moses, and the slaves
> his suffering and stubborn team.
>
> Then in his evening camp beneath
> the half-light pillars of the trees
> he filled the steepled cone of night
> with shouted prayers and prophecies.
>
> While past the camp fire's crimson ring
> the star-struck darkness cupped him round,
> and centuries of cattlebells
> rang with their sweet uneasy sound.
>
> Grass is across the waggon-tracks,
> and plough strikes bone beneath the grass,
> and vineyards cover all the slopes
> where the dead teams were used to pass.
>
> O vine, grow close upon that bone
> and hold it with your rooted hand.
> The prophet Moses feeds the grape,
> and fruitful is the Promised Land.

The impact of this is rich and immediate. We shall see what

is distinctive about it if we compare it with 'The Stockman', by
David Campbell, a poet of Miss Wright's own age:

> The sun was in the summer grass,
>   The coolibahs were twisted steel:
> The stockman paused beneath their shade
>   And sat upon his heel,
> And with his reins looped through his arm
> He rolled tobacco in his palm.
>
> His horse stood still. His cattle dog
>   Tongued in the shadow of the tree,
> And for a moment on the plain
>   Time waited for the three.
> And then the stockman licked his fag
> And Time took up his solar swag.
>
> I saw the stockman mount and ride
>   Across the mirage on the plain;
> And still that timeless moment brought
>   Fresh ripples to my brain:
> It seemed in that distorting air
> I saw his grandson sitting there.

We can see straightaway the immense difference; and it is a
difference, not only in technique, but also in the way of *con-
ceiving* the subject-matter. Although superficially the subject-
matter of both poems is very similar, their content in point of
fact could hardly differ more, simply because their attitudes to
their subject are so different. For Campbell, the stockman is an
element in a certain kind of Australian landscape – the bleak,
bare kind. The stockman himself is rather bleak and bare like
the landscape, and it is only by his most trivial movements
(rolling a cigarette, for example) that we know that Campbell
is presenting us with the Australian's dream of himself; an
independent, tough, hard-eyed, courageous type, who fits into
his landscape so well that the issue of his struggle to subdue it
can scarcely be in doubt. The whole presentation is shallow,
because it is based on a cliché; and its tone is toughly whimsical,
bordering on sentimentality.

When we turn back to Miss Wright's poem we cannot help
being struck by its superiority in richness and suggestiveness.
The first reason, I think, is that she has harnessed her lyrical
impulse to the purposes of a quite formal statement. The poem

is full of colour and movement, but it is colour and movement stilled, stylized, until the picture which it presents is seen to be of a significance as deep as those in the Old Testament. The bullocky is representative of his class, he does the ordinary work of a bullocky; and in so doing, he is laying the first supply lines of a nation. But his role is thus in some sense sacred, all the more so because of the terrific toll which it exacts from him. In order to represent these three aspects of his life – his representative quality, the sacred character of his pioneering, and the hardships which it causes – Judith Wright adopts the device of presenting him as a madman, a particularly lurid case of religious mania. He imagines that he is Moses, that his bullocks are slaves, and that the bush track is the way from Egypt into the Promised Land. By adopting this rather daring device, she is in danger of making him simply a bizarre character, without any reference to Australian conditions at all. It is a danger which she meets splendidly; and she meets it by keeping an unwavering balance between the bullocky's biblical imagination and his ordinary day-to-day pioneering.

The effect is to give both richness and universality to the bullocky, while not permitting her readers to forget the Australian setting. Words like 'camp fire' and 'cattlebells' keep us firmly anchored to our own country even while they are being used to suggest the traditional nature of the bullocky's pioneering efforts. And even though it was the old man's madness which persuaded him that he was Moses, his claim receives an endorsement from Miss Wright at the end of the poem. He has, in fact, played the symbolic role of Moses in the establishment of a new promised land:

> O vine, grow close upon that bone
> and hold it with your rooted hand.
> The prophet Moses feeds the grape,
> and fruitful is the Promised Land.

Nature, then, even while she is implacable in her destruction of those who attempt to make use of her, is capable of responding to the needs of a later generation. The pioneers are doomed; nature will not endure them; but their progeny, whether mystical or actual, may gain from the initial defeat. What happens, of course, is not that nature gives up the battle, but that human sacrifice in some cases may enable man to win that battle. Miss Wright deserves our gratitude for stating her issues so plainly, and for refusing to be distracted by the outback sentimentalism into which such a good poet as Campbell occasionally falls.

Her most loving responsiveness to nature is seen in the poems, such as 'For New England', where she speaks of her intimate identification with the countryside of her birth. It is only when Australia is seen as a natal land that Miss Wright can love it, instead of merely fearing or, at the best, tolerating it. It is worth noticing, too, that the natal land is for the poet a blend of two traditions:

> Your trees, the homesick and the swarthy native,
> blow all one way to me, this southern weather
> that smells of early snow . . .

She deserves our gratitude for this as well: for reminding us that an enthusiastic nativism is not enough; that a full response to Australia is a response to 'the double tree', to European culture and Australian strength working together, personalized in the one person and love.

Even though the mood of loving optimism is only occasional, it has admitted of a certain development, a real deepening. 'Train Journey' is, in this respect, superior to 'For New England'. The recreation of landscape is made in deeper and more satisfying terms:

> Glassed with cold sleep and dazzled by the moon,
> out of the confused hammering dark of the train
> I looked and saw under the moon's cold sheet
> your delicate dry breasts, country that built my heart;
>
> and the small trees on their uncoloured slope
> like poetry moved, articulate and sharp
> and purposeful under the great dry flight of air,
> under the crosswise currents of wind and star.

It is obvious what is happening here. In 'Bullocky', the Australian landscape was a colourful, almost apocalyptic setting for a human drama of great symbolic importance. Here, on the other hand, it is the landscape itself which is humanized: it is the Australian land and its various growths which carry the symbolic meaning. The contours of the country seem like 'delicate dry breasts'; and the trees are as 'articulate and sharp and purposeful' as poetry. Miss Wright's feeling for her native soil has found its expression in an identification between the land's body and the human body, while the land's significance is given in terms of the highest human activities and aspirations. Landscape is imperceptibly becoming human. It is notable, too, that this particular recreation of the land is made possible at a moment when the poet is in a very real sense divorced from it.

> Glassed with cold sleep and dazzled by the moon,
> out of the confused hammering dark of the train. . .

This may or may not mark an advance in understanding on the poet's part. I am inclined to think that the kind of treatment given here will not bear very much repetition. Yet it certainly marks an advance in responsiveness, in the development of sensibility. And although the strain is too occasional, it is an unusually compelling one.

While she sees nature as the context for, or the symbol of, purposive human activity, Miss Wright steps momently among the finest poets of our generation, in Australia or anywhere else; for then she writes as a woman. Yet she does so only too seldom. When nature is seen as implacable force, or as the determinant of the human process, or as a pattern of images for abstracted contemplation, it all becomes in the end rather frightening or rather boring.

I have already said, or at least hinted, something of the nature of her themes; and it is necessary to say more. For in the work of such a poet the themes are primary; they are not mere excuses for generating a brood of unrelated images. They are constant and central; and they reveal something which we are justified in calling an attitude to life.

I should say that the advance in maturity which is perceptible between *The Moving Image* and *Woman To Man*, and which has largely been retracted in the period between *Woman To Man* and *The Gateway,* is an advance in spiritual depth rather than in technique. Naturally enough, it has had its influences on her technique; but in itself it is primarily a spiritual one. We may see this by comparing the themes and attitudes expressed in the various books.

The motto of her first collection is Plato's 'Time is a moving
image of eternity'. But this motto, whatever Miss Wright under-
stands by it, does not seem to be borne out by the poems themselves. It seems, in fact, to be contradicted by them. In almost
every poem there is a good deal about time; but there is nothing
about eternity at all. The theme of almost every poem is the
frighteningly precise way in which Time can, and inevitably
does, it seems, lead to agony or decay. Time is thus seen as an
enemy, appearing under different guises in different poems. In
one it is an

>   hour
> that like a bushranger held its guns on us
> and forced our choice

In another, it is 'a gilt clock that leaked the year away'. In yet
others, it takes the form of an agonizing wind, or of a deadly
snake, 'Time sprang from its coil and struck his heart'.

It is capable of destroying the grace of the old squatters just
as easily as it destroyed the ancient grace of aboriginal civilization. It brings on wars, and leaves people no spiritual defence
against their ravages. It causes erosion of the land just as surely
as it causes erosion of the human heart. It is a destructive force,
against which Miss Wright in her poetry is raising an anguished
protest.

As we have seen, there is a good deal of vitality in the poems
in *The Moving Image*. But it cannot really be described as a
vitality springing from hope, or from the perception of a final
purpose in the workings of the world. The passion and colour
with which she presents her situations are the product as much
of her sense of failure – even of despair – as of the fresh response
of her senses to the vitality of nature. In almost all her poems,
in this first volume, at least, she quite explicitly leaves no hope
of redemption. All her characters – if we may call them characters – are frustrated in some way by life and time; and she
leaves little doubt that the frustration in each case is not a
temporary, but an all-too-permanent one. The songs of dingoes
and aborigines are gone forever, no matter how heroic the one
or how sacred the other. She sees little hope for wartime lovers,
for Air Force pilots, for idlers and aged settlers. In 'Remittance
Man', she is able to become ironic about the meaninglessness of
it all:

That harsh biblical country of the scapegoat
closed its magnificence finally round his bones
polished by diligent ants. The squire his brother,
presuming death, sighed over the documents,
and lifting his eyes across the inherited garden
let a vague pity blur the formal roses.

It is true that, in this poem, Miss Wright is concerned to show
one way of life as against another; and the richness of phrasing
which results from this opposition will probably be the first thing
to catch the reader's eye. But it cannot altogether conceal the
hopelessness beneath the irony.

At the end of 'The Moving Image' itself she cries out for a
new world and a new song; but the cry comes at the end of a
series of images suggesting death, aridity, distortion, and madness; and, even considered apart from its context, it has a
frenzied note. In 'The Hawthorn Hedge', despite the scene of
domestic courage, she shows us a hedge whose only real use is
that the ageing woman can hide behind it – presumably from
the world.

The point of all this, of course, is that Judith Wright feels herself – not only knows herself – to be involved in the universal
mystery of agony and decay. Fear of time is only one aspect of
her fear of the whole natural process, which I noted before. She
is by no means a professional pessimist, breaking into song only
to remind us what a bad way the world is in. But we must not
forget that her bent is lyrical, that her responses to experience
are immediate and colourful, and that these responses tend to
formulate themselves into images rather than statements. What
strikes her lyrist's sensibility with great force is the co-presence
in all experience of richness and decay, with agony or madness
sometimes arising from the process of decay. Her senses and
emotions register these opposites together, but because of a lack
of any fixed belief, or because of the immaturity that will not
endure serenity, her mind tends to stress the decay. At times she
tries, wearily or frenziedly, to speak of a new richness springing
from the decay of the old, but she cannot bring herself really to
imagine it, and so it does not act as a solvent of the conflict.
What *does* happen quite often is that we notice the lyrical
richness on the surface of the poetry, and are so struck by it that

we notice nothing else. In other words, her lyrical gifts tend to gloss over, or to neutralize, the effect of her own attitudes.

And, after all, the anguish over time is a constant theme in modern poetry. Time, cries that non-existent monster, 'the average modern poet', is the enemy of everything; and he gives the word a capital letter in consequence. I do not think we ought to confuse this attitude with that of Shakespeare's Sonnets, or with the rueful sensuality of 'Gather ye rosebuds while ye may'; the whole point of the attitude I am discussing is that while one may look at the rosebuds, even agonize over them, Time will not let them stay to be gathered. And even such a good poet as Judith Wright is deeply affected by this attitude.

In the opening poems of *Woman to Man*, the pessimistic drift is arrested, the conflict finds a solvent. More than that: it finds its own meaning. The emphasis of these extraordinary and lovely poems is not only on the almost sacramental quality of sexual love, but on the mystical significance of love as a means for the transmission of life. It is the finest poetry I know by any woman – and it is also, in a real sense, the most womanly. But the balance she achieves there is as temporary in its influence on her work as it is compelling in its immediacy. The child once born, the rapture of love is dissipated, the sense of the unity of human experience is broken. The poet lapses into an isolation of 'prophecy' as complete as the earlier isolation of despair.

So the motto of her last collection, *The Gateway*, is a passage from Blake, and the passage itself is an earnest of what Miss Wright now considers her poetic function to be:

> Thou perceivest the Flowers put forth their precious Odours;
> And none can tell how from so small a centre comes such sweet,
> Forgetting that within that centre Eternity expands
> Its ever-during doors . . .

Her new task is to find the general in the particular. Not, I must insist, to deduce the general from the particular, but to see it in the particular. She now considers herself a symbolist; she deals in the currency of the old, almost magical archetypal symbols, the lion, star, moon, Eden, desert, blood; and her technique in minting is derived heavily from Blake and Yeats.

The result is a bit of a hotch-potch. I have always felt that, considering the rather narrow range of her themes and central images, she writes too much. *The Gateway,* as a collection, gives notice that she is straining the poetic blood-vessel with too constant an agitation. She is trying to maintain herself too long and too often at fever point, the point of inspiration, the point at which symbolic reflection is possible; and I feel that, in consequence, she is not contemplating the particular deeply enough; she is sketching it in and attempting to wrench the general from it. The result is disturbingly like the creation of a world of 'symbols' – or, more simply, high-sounding images – for their own sake.

Every now and again it comes off; it does, for example, in 'Lion':

> Lion, let your desert eyes
> turn on me.
> Look beyond my flesh and see
> that in it which never dies;
>
> that which neither sleeps nor wakes –
> the pool of glass
> where no wave rocks or breaks,
> where no days or nights pass.
>
> Your shining eyes like the sun will find
> an image there
> that will answer stare for stare
> till with that gaze your gaze is blind.

This is a fine poem, though its movement is perhaps a little hasty. But when we look at 'Botanical Gardens', we find a desperate reliance on technique, and on technique alone, which reveals almost a cynical attitude to poetry:

> Under the miraculous baptism of fire
> that bows the poinciana tree, the old man drab as a grub
> burrows with his spade. Alas, one's whole life long
> to be haunted by these visions of fulfilled desire.

The name for this kind of thing is spiritual melodrama. She is now writing a standard product, repeating the same poem time and again in cadences which are, as often as not, ill chosen. This trait seems to me to be connected, either as a result or cause, with another – with one of her typical defects. Wherever Miss Wright shows a major weakness of execution, it seems to arise from a straining after effect, and to issue in melodrama of one

kind or another. In various poems in *The Moving Image*, we
have statements like this:

> The hard enquiring wind strikes to the bone
> and whines division . . .

The wind is unaccountably versatile – so much so, in fact, that
it is able to do several things at once. This, however, is prentice
work; the weakness can be explained by saying that a young
poet is trying too hard. By the time we get to *The Gateway*, we
find a more seriously disabling kind of lapse – a lapse caused by
the fact that she is using her key ideas and images as talismans.
The idea is this: 'When you hear the theme music strike up,
you know that an important spectacle is going to be presented
for your edification and uplift':

> The orange-tree that roots in night
> draws from that night his great gold fruit,
> and the green bough that stands upright
> to shelter the bird with the beating heart.
>
> Out of that silent death and cold
> the tree leaps up and makes a world
> to reconcile the night and day,
> to feed the bird and the shining fly –
>
> a perfect single world of gold
> no storm can undo nor death deny.

It would be rash to say that this was meaningless; but we
ought, I think, to remark that it is a piece of wishful thinking –
a fancy not far removed from the order of fairy-tale piety. It is
pretty, of course, in its way; but the prettiness is a surface one,
a collection of nice and unimportant images.

To put the point in another way, whenever Miss Wright loses
sight of the object as a thing in itself, she tends to stop writing
poetry and to start making vague gestures in the direction of a
cosmic symbolism which does not seem to mean very much,
either to us or to herself. I would go further, and say that she
loses sight of the object whenever she ceases to gaze at it with
the eyes of an immediate personal emotion. This is a tendency
constant in all three books. When she is content to be a woman,
enduring the profound incidents of a woman's life, she is able,
paradoxically enough, to transcend her womanliness and be a
very fine poet. When she attempts to be not a woman, but a

bard, commentator or prophet, she becomes a bit of a shrew—
which is the worst and most unwomanly of all things that a
woman can become. The temptation is not, of course, insur-
mountable, but the critics have given Miss Wright no help in
surmounting it. As a matter of fact, they have written on the
tacit assumption that she is somehow beyond criticism. One
recent critic has actually said that Judith Wright is 'beyond
criticism'.

This is on the level of Dr Johnson's remark made on a similar
matter; that the wonder is not that she does it so well, but that
she can do it at all. And, whether stated or implied, it is an
attitude dangerous to Miss Wright's poetic development.

Her powers, then, are very considerable. They consist of a
brilliance of image, a rhetorical facility which assists her in her
image-making, an elevated sense of her mission both as woman
and poet, and a strikingly strong lyrical impulse. Her experience
of man's life and of the natural world is a rich one; and in her
best poems it is presented in a direct, vital way, without the
myriad hesitations and circumlocutions which so many modern
poets use, from fear of looking too closely at the human state.
When all these powers act together as agents of the one immediate and personal emotion, we get a very fine and exciting
poetry. Yet, apart from a few powerful and homogeneous poems
in *Woman to Man*, they have acted together all too seldom.[1]
What is missing, in her otherwise compelling first book, is a
sufficiently broad range of emotions and a sufficiently individual
note. What is missing, in her otherwise glittering third book, is
a sufficient sense of her own humanity, and of the humanity of
others. Seldom do we find in either of these books the perfectly
inflected tone of the speaking voice giving balance and emphasis
to an elevated statement of love. We find it in abundance in
Woman to Man:

> I wither and you break from me;
> yet though you dance in living light
> I am the earth, I am the root,
> I am the stem that fed the fruit,
> the link that joins you to the night.

[1] At least one exception (and it is a notable one) must be made in favour
of 'The Harp and the King,' a recent poem of great power and meaning which,
despite the fact that it reveals an emphasis unusual in Miss Wright's poetry,
touches her finest work.

Her weaknesses, too, are as obvious as her proficiencies; and they seem to arise from three separate but complementary sources: From too great a reliance on (even imitation of) other poets; from a confusion of themes and attitudes coming from her own confusion of aim, which results first in a pessimism of which the cause is inadequately defined, and secondly in the too facile optimism of the person who is a contemplative-at-will; and from a straining after original or forceful effects plus a reliance on her own facility as a maker of images. The balance is undoubtedly in her favour. She is a real poet, a poet in the mainstream of our English and Australian poetry, a poet, perhaps, with a capital 'P'. It would be stupid to pretend that she is merely of the usual run of minor poets; it is equally stupid, and even dangerous, to overestimate her. For, as much as anyone else, she demands of us an estimate of what she has already achieved, and some sort of statement on the final tendencies of her work.

Classicism and Grace: James McAuley

JAMES McAULEY is a younger and probably more controversial representative than A. D. Hope of that tendency in modern Australian poetry which may be called at once humanist and classical. Although he was born as late as 1917, I am quite sure that the term 'controversial' is a correct one to apply to him, and that it has been applicable for some years. After all, most people will refuse to start controversies unless they are forced to do so, or unless they are sure of winning: and far more than his friend Hope, McAuley has (and without intending it) forced controversy about himself. He has done this first by the comparatively simple device of publishing a book – a book which contains some very good poetry indeed; secondly, by the relatively more complicated business of engaging in a literary hoax which shattered some dearly-held reputations; and, last of all, by remaining a 'Classicist' and becoming a Catholic. And he has managed all this despite the fact that very few of the people who consider him most controversial have ever seen him. Nevertheless, it can be positively stated that he does exist; he is as real as Ern Malley.

McAuley as a poet is concerned with romantic love and with the action of social forces; he is also concerned, and in a way which hardly exercises Hope's imagination at all, with the meaning of his own inner states. I shall be returning to each of these themes and preoccupations as they are to be found in his mature poetry.

Before I do so, however, it will be necessary to make a couple of preliminary remarks. When, in an age like this, one calls a poet a Classicist, one ought to consider it just as important to avoid question-begging as to eschew glib definition. McAuley was educated in the University of Sydney; and I have recently scanned certain issues of the magazine *Hermes* to see what kind of poetry he published there as an undergraduate. I did so not through any antiquarian obsession, but in order to follow out a suspicion which the reading of his later work had engendered in me. And I found that what had most exercised McAuley the undergraduate was a romantic rebellion, seemingly against the dour necessities of life itself. It was a rebellion compounded equally of fierceness and irony, of realistic analysis and romantic yearning, of an urge to self-expression and an urge to self-laceration in the very act of expression. McAuley, in fact, was the very type of the Joycean intellectual; in some moods, I think it is sufficient to say, of the modern intellectual. His poem 'In Honour of Chris. Brennan' may go some distance towards proving the point; it has been reworked twice, until in its present form it bears not the slightest resemblance to the original which is printed here:

(i)

Who knows what tidal impulse sweeps
The unimagined tumult of the blood?
His soul is good that on its centre rides,
Faithless he knows the limits of control
And secret sits above the flood.

Peace will come only when the veins subside
To them whose fates are not shut up or spent;
And of that shrunken turmoil what remains,
What offering? – Who shall deride?
Perhaps a verse, a fireside ornament.

(ii)

See from the train. Recumbent suburbs turn
A face that's Nubian upon earth's shoulder,
Freckled with light.
Cramped yellow copy of the face of night!
No spheres; no cherubim; and so much older
Seems than the original, the august, height.

Earth-minds are vague in those dark corridors,
Unconscionable menace, echo's absence,
Defends the silent seas and continents
From the torn sail of a conquistador.

Seen from afar,
This too no glory has but of a star;
But not that heaven of galaxies is worth
One Genius' window, bright with lamp of earth.

One of the interesting things about this early piece is the fact that it establishes a strain which seems to be constant in McAuley's poetry – at least until its most recent development.

That is the strain of the rhetorical gesture, a gesture striving always to be not vague and self-defeating, but rather general and graceful at once, sensuous perception striving to become either mime or music. For the present, however, I am more interested in other things about it. It establishes beyond the slightest doubt that the later position to which McAuley came was earned by struggle, made firm by a process of self-purification rather than by any easy assumption of its rightness. It establishes, too, that his classicism (for so we must no doubt continue to call it) is a matter not of cold formalism and of withdrawal from life, but of a realism at once personal, social, and philosophical. We are not to look to McAuley for a poetry of simple moral statement, still less of sententiousness, but for a poetry in which the anguish which engendered it remains, albeit sublimated and given a different order of appeal. I say that these qualities 'are' there, even though it must be confessed that McAuley's whole approach has changed enormously over the past ten years, and that the dominant qualities of his poetry have changed with it to a degree most unusual among genuine artists.

The only book which he has so far published is entitled *Under Aldebaran,* and was published in 1946. It is an uneven book, both in the quality of the poetry and in the positions or attitudes which it states. Some of the poems in it seem to me comparatively worthless, and it is not necessary to devote marked attention to them; what is more disturbing is that certain of them are in danger of undermining the completeness and maturity of the position, the cast and quality of life, which he adopts in the really fine poems. The silliness and incipient bathos of 'Rhyme's End', the rather pointless cynicism of 'Dialogue', the Freudian inconsequence of much of the sequence known as 'The Family of Love'—all these things cannot help proving unwelcome in a book which includes 'Gnostic Prelude', 'Autumn', 'The Celebration of Love' and 'The Incarnation of Sirius'. The two groups seem to belong to two different and mutually exclusive worlds of imagination. They may probably be joined only in the light of a deeper temperament, a more radical revolt, than appears on the surface. Nevertheless, this seeming incompatibility of temperaments is probably due to

McAuley's youth; he was barely twenty when some of these poems were written. And I shall be concerning myself with the better poetry, on the grounds that the attitudes displayed in the worse are not at all important ones, and do not finally affect our judgment of his poetic output.

The particular theme of these poems seems to be that of discovery. 'Chorale' treats of the discovery by the poet of the recurring surges of life in him which provide the materials of his art. 'Celebration of Love' treats of the discovery by a pair of lovers of the archetypal meanings of their love; and similar things might be said about a number of the other poems.

But it is necessary, in this matter, to be both more precise and more inclusive. One half of McAuley's poetic sensibility reaches out towards the general, to treat in symbolic terms the movements of society or the values which concern all men; the other half reaches deeper into itself in order to find out the meanings of its own experience. In both operations, he is engaged in kinds of discovery, and in neither kind does the process itself reach any definitive resolution within the scope of *Under Aldebaran*.

In the more general poems, he makes an affirmation and an attack—an affirmation of the values which give real life and real stability to society, and an attack on the factors, whether they be institutions or human attitudes, which thwart those values, and which, moreover, set up false images of life and a false stability: in 'The Blue Horses', we see this opposition made explicit and even dramatic:

> Progeny of winds, sea-forms, earth-bestriders,
> From the blue quarries of their natal hills
> Terribly emerging to their riders,
> Blue Horses lift their neighing trumpets to the moon!
> They stamp among the spiritual mills
> That weave a universe from our decay:
> The specious outline crumbles at the shock
> Of visionary hooves, and in dismay
> Men hide among the tumbled images.
>
> The silver trumpets strike the moon!
> O grasp the mane with virgin hand:
> Beneath the knocking of the magic hoof
> New spaces open and expand.

We see that the forces of life must first be forces of destruction.

And what is to be destroyed? McAuley himself gives us part
of the answer; in a note appended to this poem, he states that the
'Blue Horses' 'seemed to me a symbol of that animal imaginative
passion which creates the forms of a culture but will not rest
in them, eternally invoking chaos against the simplifications of
reality on which custom depends'. Custom, that is, depends on a
pattern of illusions, of refusals and falsifications. It is the natural
habitat of minds which refuse recognition to the primitive forces
in the personality, which deny the force of poetic vision, and
which, while being attuned to cruelty and hate, give themselves
a false security, a security based on a lie:

> Possess!
> All things escape us, as we too escape.
> We have owned nothing and have no address
> Save in the poor constriction
> Of a legal or poetic fiction.
> He that possesses is possessed
> And falsifies perception lest
> The visionary hooves break through
> The simple seeming world he knew.
> Possess!
> His wife hangs lace across the view
> And all they know of lucid lithe Septembers
> Is guilty dreams and itching members.

So far, we are being given the analysis typical of a man who
is both something of an anarchist and something of a vitalist;
and the forces which destroy the orders of custom are seen as
naturalistic ones, working through society largely by the instrument of war, but largely independent of man's will.
McAuley seems to be saying that if you expel nature with a
weaver's loom and a fountain pen she will come back in the
guise of a vengeful Mars, having conveniently changed her sex
in the period of her exile. Even those who feel his anger justified
may find the rational analysis of its causes inadequate. This is
because it is not yet properly associated with positive spiritual
forces, and in particular with the assertion of poetic vision. It is
a protest certainly powerful enough, but too negative and
naturalistic to be satisfying; too confused, perhaps, to appeal
permanently to an adult mind.

In other poems, the protest is carried further. McAuley does not work only through direct statement and through images common to a minority group, as so many of the Left-Wing or the *Bulletin* poets do; he takes symbols which are unusual yet capable of being recognized by the educated reader, and invests them with a personal feeling, puts them into a context of images always personal, and sometimes bordering on the private or cryptic. One of these is the symbol of Mercator, the merchant, who has put his own interpretation on human experience, until we get throughout society a false spiritual projection akin to that of the mapmakers who follow Mercator's Projection. As he says, with an ironic parody of passion, in 'The Family of Love':

> The world's the thing; Mercator its false prophet;
> We scramble on a flat projection of it.
> But oh the foggy Greenlands of the soul!
> The monstrous malformations round the Pole!

This is a piece of symbolism which we might have expected McAuley to seize on with his quick mind and to endow with his passionate scorn. Mercator is the prophet of a world living by false standards, making (and for comfort's sake) the rounded, the full, the passionate, into a flat and over-simplified sketch. He is a merchant, but he is also a planner; above all, he is a Judas, who will betray the world into the arms of the avenger.

Opposed to the false prophet you have the true; and it is in his affirmation of life's revenge on its traducer that McAuley rises to the heights of a poetry at once lyrical and eloquent. The world which lives by Mercator's projection is submitted at once to the judgment and the transforming power of history itself and of the passionate, life-affirming individual. History (which McAuley would probably not endow with the royal prerogative of the capital H, as I am doing) makes its judgment felt through fratricidal war; and the cosmic order of the stars and planets assists it in its work of cleansing. In all this, the cowardice of the life-denying world turns to positive evil; the Augean Stables breed their own armed men. This seems to be the theme of that remarkable and partly obscure poem 'The Incarnation of Sirius':

> But at its showing forth, the poets cried
> In a strange tongue; hot mouths prophesied
> The coolness of the bloody vintage-drops:
> 'Let us be drunk at least, when the world stops!'

Anubis-headed, the heresiarch
Sprang to a height, fire-sinewed in the dark,
And his ten fingers, bracketed on high,
Were a blazing candelabra in the sky.

The desert lion antiphonally roared;
The tiger's sinews quivered like a chord;
Man smelt the blood beneath his brother's skin
And in a loving hate the sword went in.

But this is an apocalyptic vision, obscure in certain of its details. In calmer and less world-delivering mood, McAuley sees help and judgment alike coming through history by the action of the truly spiritual man. Such a one is Henry of Portugal, Henry the Navigator, whose championship of his own adventurous captains is calm and sure, a Biblical courage come again:

The Navigator saw no distant seas,
Yet guided ships: his spirit went with them
Much like that going in the mulberry trees
Which roused the Israelites up off their knees
And gave them faith, direction, stratagem.

It may be apposite here to anticipate a later part of these reflections and to say that the Navigator's qualities are echoed in the qualities of the poetry itself. What is most noticeable about it is the intellectual and poetic authority with which the poet draws his conclusion. There is neither hedging nor shuffling; because of the sureness with which he has grasped both his thought and its implications, McAuley's passion (one might almost say, crusading passion) seems a model of classical serenity. Like his own devout hero, he is able to give 'direction, stratagem' to his poetic line.

But so far I have been dealing, and dealing very sketchily, at that, with his analysis of society in general. Something remains to be said of the other great preoccupation in *Under Aldebaran* – the attempt to discover the meaning of his own inner states, and in particular of the inner processes which beget poetry. We must notice that the way in which McAuley poses this question to himself is very far from the impressionistic excitement and self-congratulation of the Romantic. He really is trying, by a sort of personal depth-analysis, to see what are the archetypal meanings of the poetic process. The poetic spirit is represented

by the sun, which can irradiate consciousness only at the cost
of recurrent withdrawal into the subconscious. Self-discovery
must precede contemplation of the external world:

> At night the sun walks underneath the waves
> And like a diver in a diving-bell
> Illuminates the ooze and ocean caves,
> Each snag of coral and each triton shell.
>
> His eastward path is through these liquid walks,
> Clouded with tiny coloured fish and swarms
> Of glass medusae, where amid polyp-stalks
> The octopus conceals his strangling arms.
>
> Yet while his golden energy is drowned
> His sister moon performs her transmutation
> Converting it to silver triple-crowned,
> As human lust is changed to contemplation.

It is the marriage of heaven and hell which all poets must
make; and the courage and vision required to make it are the
best champions of that spirit in history which defies Mercator's
world:

> The universe becomes an algebraic
> Choir of symbols, dance and counterdance,
> Colours and forms in shimmering mosaic:
> Man enters it as an inheritance.

Such a universe is not the poet's alone, it belongs to all men;
and by engaging in the labour of self-discovery necessary to
reveal it, the poet is working as a representative of all mankind.
That is his peculiar glory, as the effort of self-discovery needed
to achieve it is his risk, his occupational hazard:

> O seraph in the soul, who singing climb
> The orders of creation as a stair,
> And hold a silver lamp above the time
> And places of our deepening despair:
>
> When the delirium swirls within the gyre,
> And comets die, and iron voices wake,
> Be witness to the sun; and mounting higher
> Hold the lamp steady, though creation shake.

The poet is entitled to his exultation, as he is irrevocably committed to his risk. And the exultation which this poem professes,
and of which it is a splendid example, is one achieved momen-

tarily, almost fortuitously, and certainly only at the expense of great effort on the part of its author. In addition to this, it looks forward to new dangers, new and oppressive 'deaths' and 'deliriums', in the face of which it is to give a continuing strength to the poetic soul. It is a rather desperate exultation, which shows a consciousness of the fact that the poet's career is largely at the mercy of impersonal forces which he cannot control. The same is true of much of the other poetry in *Under Aldebaran;* wherever exultation appears, it is an exultation hardly won and mixed with intimations of the possibility of despair. Wherever we find rage and scorn, we find them directed at himself and his own precarious vocation as much as at human folly; rage is of.en, in McAuley's poetry, an index to a hidden fear; and it cannot be vented in the impersonal tone of commentary which so much poetry demands. Despite the persistent care for control, for precision of statement and clarity of image, the poet seems to be fighting a continual rearguard action – against the menace of history and the frightening demands of his own nature. Wherever anything is gained, it has had to be fought for; and the battleground was the personality itself of the poet.

I do not know if McAuley would still be prepared to advance this conception of poetry as a sort of edifying adventure. Certainly, if his rather shoddy satirical poem, 'A Letter to John Dryden', may be adduced in evidence, he would now completely reject that view, derived from Blake and Jung, of the relationship between the imagination and the subconscious which gives point to such poems as 'Chorale'. And certainly, his later poetry shows a marked change in emphasis, a new feeling of subjective freedom. We may see this if we look at any of the lyrics written since his conversion to Catholicism:

> The wagtail in the myrtle-tree
> Who cannot sleep for love
> Sings all night long insistently
> As if his song could prove
> What wisdom whispered from the start,
> That only love can fill the heart.
>
> He sang under the boughs of youth,
> Through twisted shadowed years;
> He sings in this clear night of truth,

And now my spirit hears;
And sees, when beating wings have done,
The lucid outline of the Swan.

The exultation here is one of release – a liberation not so much of one precarious and menaced impulse as of a whole personality. It is more lovely than the 'Chorale', but in a more obvious way; it lacks tension, and the power which tension often gives to a poetic line; and it lacks too that sense, which delights us even in the simplest of great lyrics, the sense that language is being used creatively, that words are being recreated through their use in this one poem. We might say that, since it is a released poetry, it is also to some extent a disembodied poetry.

Yet it is true that McAuley has found a new use for poetry – a use of which he had scarcely been aware previously. Poetry may now be used to praise; it is seldom used to propagandize. Since he has become a Catholic, he has sought to make his poetry perform the double function of helping him to place the movement of his past life into a new perspective, and to give a new lyrical context to traditional images in which, during the years of Christendom, the traditional truths had been expressed and embodied. Indeed, all the poetry which he has written since the publication of his first book seems to me to be an attempt, on two different levels, to objectify and make new sense of the problems which so exercised him in his earlier development. This attempt, of course, takes in both 'context' and 'form', and it is precisely in its inclusiveness, I should suggest, that the danger of this kind of poetry lies.

First, we have the series of Greek poems called 'The Hero and the Hydra' – a series of which the best-known example is 'Prometheus', first published in *Meanjin* in 1948. In these poems, McAuley seems to be trying to 'distance' himself from his own poetic experience, to give that experience both a general application to the affairs of man and a stability derived from its roots in Greek myth. The myths of Prometheus, of Chiron, and of Heracles are revived in order to provide a framework within which the dilemma of modern man can become intelligible. I must confess that I am allergic to this kind of mythologizing. It seems to me to provide a danger to the very intelligibility which it seeks to establish; and it seems, at the same time, to commit the poet to a use of poetic forms which are in themselves debilitating. There are some lovely passages in these poems; 'Prometheus', for example, contains some of the most forceful and balanced writing McAuley has yet done; but surely the images in which a myth is revived will compel man's assent to their content only if the myths themselves are adequate to express man's sense of his own dilemma. Myths must express a genuine belief before they can be really effective as myth; unless they do, the realist intention behind them remains largely a private one, barely recognizable by anyone save the poet himself; and the images themselves, no matter how beautiful many of them may be in isolation, will live isolated or uneasy in the context of a poetic form which tends to a cold formalism. Myths for the modern age are effective only if the images of human action which they present are readily seen by a modern audience to be images of *their own* state. This is the big problem of the modern poet who is a 'classicist' in sympathies and in form. And in McAuley's case, one gets the impression that the mythological poems represent a sort of spiritual experiment which was left quickly behind him.

For he has outlived this phase of his development, and has passed into another phase – a phase in which the dominating impulse behind the images is not Greek, but medieval or perhaps Baroque. He is even more interested than before in the presentation of life as a ceremony; what has changed is the nature of the ceremony, and the dominant images in which it is re-enacted. Those people, like Mrs Vassilieff, who find McAuley a propagandist must be reminded that ritual is not propaganda; and such people, even though the missiles they throw are of another substance than stone, ought to be conscious that they themselves are living in glass houses.

The new strain in McAuley's poetry seems to take on two slightly different forms. The first is the simple (and often lovely) giving of praise and thanks that the poet has been permitted to discover the meaning of his life; a good example would be the lovely lyric 'Invocation':

> Compose the mingling thoughts that crowd
> Upon me to a lucid line;
> Teach me at last to speak aloud

In words that are no longer mine;
For at your touch, discreet, profound,
Ten thousand years softly resound.

I do not now revolt, or quarrel
With the paths you make me tread,
But choose the honeycomb and laurel
And walk with patience towards the dead;
Expecting, where my rest is stayed,
A welcome in that windless shade.

It is something, in any age, to walk with patience towards the dead; and it is something to have a lyrical poet say as much so beautifully. With more ambitious poetry, however, it seems to me of equal importance that one should walk there in company with the rest of the living; and this McAuley may not yet be doing. In such a poem as 'Celebration of Divine Love', he makes an attempt to marry the sacred and the secular, to use such images as will show the sacred incarnated in the secular, but transcending that in which it is incarnated:

Fled from his own disaster, he consults
The learned magi casting horoscopes
For the New Babylon. Plan by plan
They raise the scaffold of terrestrial hopes:
'For thus', they say, 'when exiled man
Disowns Jerusalem, which we destroy,
And learns to live, as the enlightened should,
The desecrated life, he will enjoy
The sweet fruition of all earthly good'.
Yet, ill at ease, his steps are led apart
Where the despised and hated remnant clings
To the old way with undivided will:
Out of the bowed darkness a voice sings
'If I forget thee, O Jerusalem . . .'
He listens; and his heart stands still.

This. too, is lovely, but with a loveliness a little too formalized and cold; it exhibits the paradox of a statement very generalized as to technique, but insufficiently general in grasp and application. Who will recognize himself in McAuley's statement of the possibilities? Some of this later poetry tends towards the hymn or canticle, and some towards a narrative structure; both of these are forms which no longer receive much public support. Like a number of other people, I am disappointed by the turn which his poetry has taken; but, so far as I am concerned, it is a relative disappointment, not an absolute one. This poetry seems to me inadequate to McAuley's fine intelligence and great lyrical grasp of the factual. The point is that a wedding of the sacred and the secular depends on the secular's being there to be married; ritual feeds not only on its own tradition but on the common life of the people as the poet experiences it and makes it his. And I cannot help feeling that his work at the moment is not sufficiently rooted in the actual: it is not quite earthy enough; there is too little flesh to afford incarnation to the word.

I have repeatedly referred to James McAuley as a classicist — often enough, perhaps, to beg or to confuse the question of what classicism is. In the first place, this particular classicist insists that poetry is more than self-expression, it is a making; it involves the emotions, certainly, but the emotions guided by the intellect; it is not random, but directed; it should strive to make clear, rather than opaquely expressive, its own images and lines of development; the excitement which it engenders should be an excitement of the intellect informing the senses; it should be both intelligent and intelligible. As McAuley himself has expressed the matter in an article, also in *Meanjin:*[1]

> If poetry is an intellectual [that is, an intuitive] act it is not a random indeterminate process but is governed by a previsioned end. It is something more than an experimental dredging of the subconscious in the hope of finds. Through whatever gropings and indecisions the mind may proceed, there must be a ruling conception by which it knows its quarry: some foresight of the work to be done, some seminal idea. Obviously I do not mean that the work must be composed before it is composed; the seed is not the grown tree; yet just as the developed structure of the tree is implicit in the seed so the poem is implicit in its concept . . .

Here we have a conception of the poem as a pattern in which is made explicit an intuition of reality. It is an idea at once ceremonial and realistic, a persuasive answer to expressionism; and it echoes, I suggest, sheer common sense. But such a classical idea expressed in McAuley's terms presupposes more than it states; it implies an order and a pattern already in existence before the poem appears, an order which is reflected or embodied

[1] Summer, 1953, vol. xii, no. 4, p. 433.

in the poem itself. This order, however, must be delved for; it is not available on demand. The 'order and good chance in the artesian heart' can be located or created only by the arduous job of sinking bores:

> And I am fitted to that land as the soul is to the body,
> I know its contractions, waste, and sprawling indolence;
> They are in me and its triumphs are my own,
> Hard-won in the thin and bitter years without pretence.
>
> Beauty is order and good chance in the artesian heart
> And does not wholly fail, though we impede;
> Though the reluctant and uneasy land resent
> The gush of waters, the lean plough, the fretful seed.

Throughout, McAuley's poetry is a very fine example of the truth of his own dictum. Some of his earlier poetry is obscure in its symbolism, but the obscurity is never caused by any indirection of intention in its author. His main virtue is his magnificent intellectual and artistic sanity. He seems never to embark on a poem unless its symbolic relationships, and the way in which those relationships express an idea, are alike clear to him. Take for example 'Celebration of Love', a poem which expresses the lover's delight in the discovery of his own unique separateness and that of his love:

> Yet you are more, being yourself; not merely
> A script of symbols where my heart can read
> Secrets of its nature and its need
> And know itself more clearly.
> You are yourself; and when we touch
> We understand the joy of being two,
> Not seeking to annihilate
> Distinction, as self-lovers do . . .

This is a poetry of statement, of a statement general, graceful and exalted; consequently, it is largely out of the main stream of modern poetry, which tends to play down statement in favour of imagery, or imagings. Yet it is more even than that; for the statement is accomplished largely by means of a symbolism derived from external nature, which has been submitted to the process of a Blakean vision, caught, stylized, and as it were converted into the figures of a verbal dance. It is not only the statement, but the imagery itself, which strives to be luminous and exact. What is to be understood, to be made clear, is the poem itself; the concepts and statements simply provide its core.

If we are to call such poetry intellectual, we had better be quite sure what we intend by the word. It is certainly not abstruse poetry, and it is philosophical in its materials rather than in its method. To clarify this point, I should like to quote two versions of a small lyric, not because I think even the finished version of it represents McAuley at his best, but because such a comparison affords a very good chance of seeing from his creative practice just what he means by intellectual control. First, here is the version which appeared in *Hermes* in 1937:

> When shall the fair
> hair on the thin scalp spilled
> (whereby the summer is not spoiled)
> suffice? Stare
>
> is more than eyes,
> smile is no doubt on lips
> (like sunrise gleam on spars of ships)
> still more than these.
>
> Love so is
> despair, being spirit too.
> Hair and eyes in love can do,
> lips can kiss.
>
> Love in minds
> works no completion,
> the agony of contemplation
> no limit finds.

And here is the final version which appears in *Under Aldebaran*, presented with the information that it was written between 1936 and 1938: in short, that it had been submitted to a radical reworking, even a complete re-visioning, within a period of months:

> When shall the fair
> Hair on the thin scalp spilled
> (Wherein the summer lies distilled)
> Suffice? A stare
>
> Is more than eyes;
> A smile appears on lips
> (Like sunrise gleam on spars of ships)
> But is more, and dies.

> Love so is
> Despair, being spirit too.
> Hair and eyes in love can do
> Lips can kiss;
>
> Five senses build
> A pentagon of pleasure:
> But mind, exceeding common measure,
> Is unfulfilled.

The second version is immeasurably the better. It has been freed of certain incidental obscurities, it has had its syntax clarified and tightened, a certain jerkiness of movement and ugliness of image have been removed; and, above all, the last stanza is completely changed, and changed in such a manner that, with one exultant cadence, it continues and completes the basic paradox of the whole poem. This paradox was previously implicit or obscured. In his revision, McAuley has clarified it and made it explicit; but he has done so not by trying directly to make his statement more logical, but rather by paying attention to the imagery and movement of the poem. If McAuley is intensely interested in 'meaning', he is not normally interested in it in any narrow sense.

It is not a passive poetry, as so much intellectual poetry is. On the contrary, it is forceful and active. Within a tight framework of images and ideas, the poet gives his line a flexible, swaying quality in which the impression of directed force is provided by the unusual yet precise use of verbs and adjectives, and by their careful placing:

> Sexes that were damned in sin
> Outward turn their quenchless eyes
> That before were fixed within
> On their gnawing miseries:
> When music sounds, the glances meet
> Gently, and forgo deceit.

The grace and accuracy of the diction cannot be faulted. When it is the instrument for effecting a marriage of clear ideas and sensuous realism in a poetic line which approaches the condition of dance, it gives us some of the best poetry ever written in this country. Its danger (and it is one to which McAuley

sometimes succumbs) is of a paradoxical kind: it is the danger
of using poetry to make intellectual points instead of enacting
living ideas. McAuley sometimes does this, not out of any great
preoccupation with profundity of meaning or with the difficulties
of communication, but rather, I think, from a certain haughtiness
towards the poem and its reader alike. Take, for example, his
pedantically phrased poem, 'Marginal Note':

> A ray of light, to an oblique observer,
> Remains invisible in pure dry air;
> But shone into a turbid element
> It throws distracting side-gleams everywhere
>
> And is diminished by what takes the eye.
> So poetry that moves by chance collision
> Scatters its brightness at each random mote
> And mars the lucid order of its vision.
>
> The purest meditation will appear
> Faint or invisible to those who glance
> Obliquely at its undeflected beam;
> The level eye receives its radiance.

As a defence or demonstration of a particular view of poetry, it
is neat and effective; as a poem in its own right, it is too neat to
be effective. Here imagery is not co-operating with and clarifying
thought, it is being coldly and deliberately *used by* thought. The
lines are so impeccable as to be stiff: and the ear, in following
them, takes on the rhythm and tone proper to the logical
demonstration of an argument.

The second reservation which I have about some of the poetry
in *Under Aldebaran* is one concerned not so much with weaknesses in the completed works themselves, as with a factor
which inclines to cramp the future development of their author.
It is, in a way, an introverted poetry. That is not to say that it
is the poetry of a complete and probably incurable introvert,
much less a narcissist; I have already paid tribute to his intellectual and artistic sanity. It is, however, to say that McAuley's
earlier poetry feeds a little too greedily for its subject-matter
upon its own processes, upon the processes of poetry. This is a
trait which it shares with the work of such poets as Harold
Stewart and Alexander Craig. No matter how forceful and

objectified it may be, a lot of it is poetry about writing poetry; there is hardly a poem in the whole book which does not have this as one of its themes.

Where his later poetry tends to arouse reservations, it is not for the same reason. Now, McAuley is tending not to the over-specialized, but to the over-simplified. The best of his most recent poetry has either a lyric beauty or a calm and authoritative eloquence which do not appear in the same way or to the same extent in his earlier. But it reads as though it had been freed of all tensions, all complexites of mire and blood. McAuley's present attitudes appear to me to be too simple, to involve too few elements of experience, to result from too short and effortless a self-probing, to lead to the finest poetry. And he seems content to let his militant and rather exclusive Catholicism remain curiously remote from the human preoccupations, the intense distresses of the world, which it is so wonderfully fitted to vivify and integrate. Despite its fervour and occasional vibrancy, this is not a fully incarnational poetry; for it seeks not to be warm in inclusion, but precise in exclusion.

One hopes that this latest phase is a transitional one, a phase of adjustment to a world of the imagination which is being seen in a new and refreshing light, and so prepared for a later creativity. So he gives promise of continuing to be one of the best poets our country has produced.

It must be obvious why I consider McAuley and his friend Hope to be important poets. Whether they will have much influence on our poetry is irrelevant; whether they can, is doubtful. They are both classicists, but they have different, and in a sense complementary qualities. And they are part of a new and necessary tradition in Australian poetry, a tradition in which the most important questions about man's fate are coming to be asked, in which a choice is presented to its readers, and in which poetic forms are being chosen to aid in the posing of those questions. However McAuley's work may develop in the future, he has given to poetry a mind and sensibility passionate, graceful, and intelligent. As all men do, he has vices corollary to his virtues; and we cannot help finding his poetry too self-concerned, too lacking in the more obvious kinds of human sympathy. I do not myself share the classical fervour of McAuley and Hope; nor do

I sympathize with the former's apparently whole-hearted rejection of those strains in poetry and life which he would no doubt label 'modernist'. Yet it is obvious that both poets have shown in their practice the proper diversity of classicism; we gain from them some hint of the fact that a fixed poetic form is not necessarily a dead mould, not even an empty vessel, but a cornucopia, a blessed horn spilling over riches which its author himself could hardly have expected to emerge from it. In such poetry, to which they both aspire, we have part of the answer to whatever is muddled in the neo-Romanticism of our half-century.

Index

196